Praise for
To You; Love, God

"Whether you greet your morning with these messages or hold them as the last thought of your evening, the gift will be the same—a sacred visitation, beautifully wrapped and presented."

—PHILIP GULLEY, author of *Living the Quaker Way*

"In *To You; Love, God,* Will Bowen infuses ordinary everyday life with extraordinary spiritual insight. As someone who is burned out on churchy language, I found sweet relief in Bowen's clear and accessible meditations on how God sees, knows, and loves us. I'm keeping this book on my nightstand."

—ELIZABETH ESTHER, author of *Girl at the End of the World*

"Like the great prophets who speak in the divine voice, Will Bowen offers daily wisdom and inspiration from God's mouth to your ear. This God will affirm you, challenge you, love you, and prod you to be the divine being you are. Each day's gem combines deep wisdom with the simplicity of a beginner's mind, brilliant insight, and a heavenly sense of humor— straight from the Source."

—DAVID ROBERT ANDERSON, author of *Losing Your Faith, Finding Your Soul*

"What a gift—sort of a spiritual vitamin to start each and every morning. Some of the messages are so profound that they have found their way laminated and into my wallet or on my desk where I can see them every day."

—M. MANARD, Gladstone, MO

"I look at life differently than I did before. Gone is the 'poor me' attitude."

—K. HILL, Morristown, TN

"I really feel like I am talking to God when I read the letters every morning. They have so helped me."

—M. Clesi, Boca Raton, FL

"The devotions lift me up beyond the daily dramas, always pointing up toward the Light and Truth that never changes."

—S. Farrow, Vancouver Island, BC

"On many occasions the messages are exactly what I need that day. Recently I have been sharing them with my teenage daughter, and she loves them!"

—S. Garland, Kansas City, MO

"I can't tell you how much *To You; Love, God* has meant to me. I read the inspired messages every morning, and what a beautiful way to begin the day. They give comfort, peace, and insight into experiencing the life God wants us all to experience."

—J. Westhoff, Green Valley, AZ

"These messages are the backbone of keeping my attitude positive and of helping me learn to accept others and myself as beings created by God."

—P. Loffstrom, Zinga, Tanzania

"The messages of *To You; Love, God* have inspired and sustained me through some of the most difficult times of my life, including a divorce and the recent sudden loss of my daughter."

—C. Pizzi, Calabash, NC

"*To You; Love, God* inspires me, makes me think, and most important, helps me appreciate all the blessings that come my way."

—D. Kelley, Clifton Park, NY

TO: YOU

Love,

GOD

TO: YOU

Love,

GOD

A YEAR OF DAILY GUIDANCE AND
INSPIRATION STRAIGHT FROM THE SOURCE

WILL BOWEN

CONVERGENT
BOOKS®

To You; Love, God
Published by Convergent Books

Hardcover ISBN 978-1-60142-689-5
eBook ISBN 978-1-60142-690-1

Copyright © 2014 by Will Bowen

Cover design by Mark D. Ford

Published in the United States by Convergent Books, an imprint of the Crown Publishing Group, a division of Random House LLC, New York, a Penguin Random House Company.

Convergent Books® and its open book colophon are registered trademarks of Random House LLC.

Library of Congress Cataloging-in-Publication Data
Bowen, Will.
  To you; love, God : a year of daily guidance and inspiration straight from the source / Will Bowen. — First Edition.
      pages cm
  ISBN 978-1-60142-689-5 — ISBN 978-1-60142-690-1 (electronic) 1. Devotional calendars. I. Title.
  BV4811.B625 2014
  242'.2—dc23

                                        2014024223

Printed in the United States of America
2024—First Edition

10 9 8 7 6 5

Special Sales
Most Convergent books are available at special quantity discounts when purchased in bulk by corporations, organizations, and special-interest groups. Custom imprinting or excerpting can also be done to fit special needs. For information, please e-mail SpecialMarkets@ConvergentBooks.com or call 1-800-603-7051.

For my mother, who taught me that God has no grandchildren, only children.

CONTENTS

INTRODUCTION

Joy is the infallible sign of the presence of God.
—Pierre Teilhard de Chardin

I felt like a plate spinner. You may remember plate spinners from early television variety programs like *The Ed Sullivan Show*. A plate spinner is an entertainer who balances individual dinner dishes atop dozens of thin, shoulder-high rods mounted into the stage. A brisk spin transforms each plate, for a time, into a gyroscopic top that seems to defy gravity as it balances on its delicate perch.

With only one plate whirling around on a single rod, it's easy to ensure that centrifugal force keeps that plate in the air. However, as additional plates are set into motion at ever-widening distances from the performer, the task of making certain that none crashes to the ground becomes increasingly more difficult.

As more and more dishes are added, the plate spinner must dash frantically about, shaking each wavering spindle to ensure that its plate remains aloft. At some point, he must either stop adding additional plates or watch helplessly as some are lost.

Chances are you've felt like a plate spinner yourself.

Every year life seems to hand us more and more plates to add to those we've already got spinning. We discover that not only do we need to keep our own plates spinning but more and more people are depending on us to spin theirs as well. We find ourselves dashing about in a mad frenzy, trying to keep parts of our lives from crashing to the ground.

As a minister, my job is to spin the spiritual plates of my congregation. In the early years at my first church, I noticed that people left Sunday services with their spiritual gyroscopes buzzing! They bounced out of church joyous, hopeful, and feeling a connection with God.

The church office was typically quiet Mondays through Wednesdays, but by Thursday and Friday our phones were lighting up with calls from people seeking prayer and guidance. Many Friday afternoons there would be a line of people outside my office awaiting counseling.

In call after call and session after session, I found that these wonderful people simply needed an infusion of spiritual confidence. They needed to know that they were safe, supported, and loved. In short, they needed their plates spun.

It seems that spiritual inspiration has a shelf life. A Sunday service may invoke new understandings, instill hope, and offer inspiration, but the bloom of that rose swiftly fades under the onslaught of negativity in our society.

As our church's attendance and influence grew, I noticed that I was becoming exhausted and overworked trying to keep everyone's plate spinning. My own plates were wobbling, and as a result, many of those who sought guidance from me were teetering and on the verge of crashing to the ground.

One day, while I plowed through a pile of e-mails, I wondered, *Wouldn't it be great if God could send everyone a daily e-mail just to remind them that he is present, that he loves them, that things are going to work out, and that they have everything they need?*

On impulse, I opened a new message screen and typed, "To You; Love, God." I then began to share as succinctly and poetically as I could what I would like to have God say to me in an e-mail if that were possible.

Inside, I felt exceedingly arrogant and unworthy of such a task. Who am I to speak for God—even if I'm attempting to make other people's lives better? Nonetheless, I sent it out to our e-mail database and soon people began to respond. Comments such as these became commonplace:

- "Thank you so much for your daily inspiring words."
- "My friend has been forwarding your most beautiful messages to my e-mail. I am always so deeply moved and inspired and always so grateful."
- "You have no idea how much these readings mean to me. They truly speak to my soul."
- "It's like you're speaking directly to me. Thank you!"
- "God bless you and all those involved in getting these pearls of love out there into the universe."
- "I love these daily e-mails!"
- "Your messages warm my heart."
- "I absolutely love these!"

Recipients began to ask who was writing the e-mails. I demurred with a shrug, saying simply, "God writes them." This satisfied no one.

One afternoon the church secretary buzzed me on the intercom to say that one of our board members, a tough old guy in his eighties, was at her desk demanding to know what book these "To You; Love, God" messages were being lifted from.

"What should I tell him?" She was near panic.

I swallowed hard. "Tell him they're not from a book. Tell him that God writes them."

I could hear her relate my message to our resident curmudgeon. A moment of silence followed. "Too bad," I heard him say. "I wanted to buy the book as a gift for all my friends."

You are now reading that book.

Over the years, these writings have dramatically improved my own life. This may sound strange, considering that technically I write them. At some point, however, I feel like I ceased to write them, and instead, they began writing me. I would sit at my computer with a particular issue or challenge in my mind and then feel my fingers begin to move as if of their own accord, typing the answers I sought, providing the guidance I needed, giving the reassurance I craved, and wrapping me in the love I desired.

Ironically, but not surprisingly, as I shared the messages that revived my own soul, people responded, "This is just what I needed to hear. Thank you!"

Today, I feel that these messages flow through me. Once I faced what I had previously considered blasphemy—that God might actually speak through me—I realized that if God is everywhere, then God is present in me. As I found God within myself, I saw God reflected back in my life.

I hope the messages in this book spin your plate.

And as you read, consider writing your own "To You; Love, God" messages to yourself about whatever issues you may be facing. That is, think of a challenge that you are experiencing and begin to write or type out what you would like God to say to you about this situation. If the challenge you are experiencing today could be seen through the vast, infinite, loving, and all-powerful eyes of God, what would God have to say?

Try this, and soon you'll begin to feel the presence of God as you embrace the truth that the spinner and the plate are one.

I Am

I am both the cause and the effect

I am at once unified and diverse

I am the beginning, middle, and end

I am the answers as well as the questions

I am the hand that reaches and the cheek
that feels its touch

I am the father as well as the child

I am life and more

I AM GOD

Awaken

You open your eyes each morning, slipping
silently from one dream into another.

As you move through your day, you seem
engaged and awake, but you are actually adrift
on a sea of your own thoughts and fears.

In fleeting moments, either through challenge
or elation, you momentarily stir, catching a
glimpse of your own perfection. Then, with an
appreciative sigh, you drift off, back into the
shadows—alive but asleep.

It is time to shake off your slumber.
It is time to open your eyes and see the world
    as I see it.
It is time to rise to the full height of your spirit
    and walk in light.

It is time for you to awaken.

JANUARY 1

To: You

Awaken to the plight of those around you. Their burden is as heavy as your own.

Awaken to their willingness to share your load and to accompany you on your path.

Awaken to the importance of what you have considered to be little things.

Awaken to the triviality of what you have considered to be big things.

Awaken to your utter and complete individuality.

Awaken to your oneness with me and with all.

Awaken to the truth that this life will someday end.

Awaken to the certainty that your life is eternal.

Love,
God

To: You

You have the power to dream and, thereby, determine your future.

You have the power to forgive and, thereby, unburden your soul.

You have the power to believe and, thereby, set the course for what will unfold.

You have the power to grow and, thereby, experience eternal youth.

You have the power to sense my presence and, thereby, know love, companionship, guidance, and acceptance.

The more you begin to explore and utilize your power, the more you awaken to the blessing your life truly is.

Love,
God

JANUARY 3

To: You

You have an epiphany. You break through to a new level of understanding. You awaken to a new realization.

Then you forget.
You spiral back to where you once were.
You fall asleep once again.

Don't fret.

The soul awakened to a new level must return once again to that level.

Be gentle and loving with yourself when you seem to be having a setback. A setback is an opportunity to remember where you no longer wish to be, thereby defining the new, higher level as your emotional home.

This is the process of your soul's awakening.
This is the process of life.

Love,
God

JANUARY 4

To: You

The sturdiest stools have three legs of equal length. No matter how you push such a stool, two of the legs align to resist your efforts and hold it upright.

Similarly, your foundation has three stable parts. You are your mind, your body, and your spirit.

If any of these three areas becomes unstable, you may wobble a bit, but the other two will sustain you until you regain your balance.

Each part of your threefold essence requires your loving attention.

Today,
 Expand your mind through reading.
 Strengthen your body through exercise.
 Cultivate your spirit through prayer.

Love,
God

JANUARY 5

To: You

Far out at sea, the crest of a wave begins to rise nearly imperceptibly above the surface of the vast blue ocean.

As the wave moves, it grows.
It forms.
It takes shape.

Once the wave is created, its course never deviates. It heads only in one direction.

Over time, the wave gets larger and larger still, rising and swelling until it is a great, rolling, thunderous mountain of water crashing to the shore.

Then, quietly and peacefully, the wave withdraws to become an indistinguishable part of the ocean once more.

Such is your life.

Love,
God

JANUARY 6

To: You

You pull up to a drive-through. Before you stands a sign announcing an array of meal selections: sandwiches, salads, sides, and more.

"May I take your order?" asks a pleasant voice.

Nearly everything on the menu looks good to you. There is much to choose from, and you are afraid of making a wrong choice. Rather than risk selecting something you may not like, you sit in line as cars go around you.

What if there is no wrong choice? Each choice will bring its result, certainly, but you can always pull around and make a different choice. Your life choices and your meal selections are rarely irrevocable.

This day, have the courage to sample something new. It just might bring a smile to your face and a kick to your step.

Now, may I take your order, please?

Love,
God

JANUARY 7

To: You

You lie on your arm, the weight of your own body restricting the flow of blood to your hand. Soon your hand falls asleep and feels numb. Over time it begins to get uncomfortable.

This discomfort causes you to roll off the arm, releasing your hand, which then tingles with a thousand little shocks as blood rushes in.

The hand was not asleep; it was simply cut off from its source.

Sometimes negative people and events can weigh your spirit down until you feel numb.

Fear not. Just as with your hand, you will experience ever-increasing discomfort until you take action to free yourself.

When you do, you may feel nervous, uncertain—as if a thousand little shocks are going through you. However, in time you will awaken to the joyous life you are meant to live.

Consider this day who or what might be cutting off your emotional supply, and do what you can to move away.

Love,
God

JANUARY 8

To: You

Life is a series of snowflakes.

Imagine watching a single snowflake as it tumbles and drifts on its way to the ground. Soon it lies at your feet, seeming indistinguishable from billions of others.

Like the snowflake, your days are each unique and pass before you only for a brief time.

Give this day the same focused attention you might a single snowflake. Don't compare it to others or wish that it were different. Celebrate whatever this day may bring.

Awaken to the fact that your days, just like snowflakes, will one day cover you completely and forever.

Open your eyes. Give full attention as this day passes before you, then release it to fall gently to your feet.

Another day, fresh and unique, is forming even now.

Love,
God

JANUARY 9

To: You

Your body and your emotions dance together.

It is difficult to know who is leading the dance and who is following.

You feel happy and then you smile.
You smile and then you feel happy.

Your body and emotional state serve as backup systems for one another.
Move like a youthful person to feel young.
Feel young and you will automatically begin to move like a youthful
     person.

Utilize whatever is most available to you to create the reality you desire.
Act like the person you wish to become, and that is how you will feel.
Feel like the person you wish to become, and you will act that way.

Either path leads to the same destination. Take the path today that is
most readily available to you.

Love,
God

JANUARY 10

To: You

Turn on a flashlight in the daytime and go outside.

Chances are, because of the brightness of the sun, you won't even be able to see the flashlight beam.

Gaze into the night sky from a place where there is no ambient light from the city. Notice how bright the stars appear.

Where there is darkness, it is easiest to see light. When things are challenging, it is easier for you to experience and see my presence.

The light of the flashlight is present regardless of how sunny the day.
The light of the stars is present regardless of the lights blazing from
   the city.
My light is present regardless of how well things seem to be going.

Whether you are in darkness or light right now, my light burns for you, illuminating your way and guiding your spirit.

Love,
God

To: You

If a bowl of berries were spilled onto the floor, you might wonder what caused the bowl to slip from your hands. You might question whether or not you were paying close enough attention. You might even blame yourself for being careless.

Such thoughts only distract you from a simple truth—it's time to pick up the berries.

In the future you may wish to question, wonder, ponder, theorize, and evaluate the causes and rationales behind whatever transpires. These are valid ways of discerning new directions in the future. Now, however, it is time to resolve what is in front of you.

Pick up the berries.

Love,
God

January 12

To: You

This moment is a grain of sand that will be added to the great sand castle that is your life.

This moment comes on the heels of a previous moment.
It precedes yet another moment.

Have you ever considered that the word *momentous*, which means "important, significant, having a bearing on the future," is founded upon the word *moment*?

Every moment is, therefore, momentous.

Every moment is important.
Every moment is significant.
Every moment sets the stage for future moments.

Make this moment momentous by giving it your full, loving attention and appreciation.

Love,
God

JANUARY 13

To: You

Imagine you woke up this morning and found that I had placed ten million dollars into your bank account.

What would you do with the money? Chances are you would buy things—vacations, clothes, jewelry, new cars, a new home, gifts for friends and family, etc.

Now imagine you awoke and found that you had lost something significant—perhaps a loved one disappeared, or you lost the ability to use a limb. Or you found that you were no longer free but were sentenced to live out your life in a prison cell.

Would you not spend all your newfound wealth to get back what you lost?

You see, my dear one, wealth is not how much money you have. Wealth is how much you possess that is more precious than money.

Take a few moments to do an accounting of the things that, if lost, you would give all the money you have and more to regain.

This day, rather than desiring only what money can buy and feeling poor, remember how wealthy you truly are.

Love,
God

JANUARY 14

To: You

The days of your life are like the breaths you take.

The day begins, brings you all that it has to offer, and then concludes.

You breathe in, receive the oxygen your body needs, and then you exhale.

Each breath is slightly different, just as each day is unique. You cannot repeat a day any more than you can repeat the same breath. You can neither breathe tomorrow's breath now nor rebreathe yesterday's breath.

When a breath is over, it is over.
When a day is over, it is finished.

You needn't worry if there will be another breath; so long as you live, the air will be there for you. So long as you live, everything you need for the next day awaits you.

Breathe as you live this day fully.
Live this day as you fully breathe.

Love,
God

To: You

When you worry, you sit downstream fretting over what the flowing current of life might bring.

What you fail to realize is that worry actually places the very thing you fear into the stream above you. Your anxious predictions then float by, and you conclude that worrying was justified.

Beloved one, know that worry anticipates; therefore, worry creates.

You were not born to worry. It was taught to you and reinforced by your own experience until it became habitual.

Begin now to create a new habit. Whenever you notice yourself beginning to worry, replace your troubling thoughts with thoughts of blessings and statements of faith.

Give thanks for what is going well. Place positive expectations into the stream above you, and know that soon—very soon—they will drift down into what you call reality.

Love,
God

JANUARY 16

To: You

For all the time you spend wondering about what might be, you miss what is, and more important, you step away from creating what can be.

It's like taking your hands off the steering wheel to ponder where your car will go.

I have given you a mind for the purpose of deciding where you want to be and what you wish to become. Certainly you came into life with talents and predilections. But to sit and wait for me to tell you the answer to "What shall I become?" is to take your hands off the wheel.

Decide.

Once the decision is made, then I will begin to construct the map to get you to your destination.

My purpose is to make certain your course is smooth and your destination is ensured. This day, make a decision as to the next stop along your journey, then sit back and enjoy the ride.

Love,
God

January 17

To: You

You can hope to someday have something, or you can declare it yours—now.

You can wonder if the future will be bright, or you can define it as you wish it to be.

You can beseech life to give you what you desire, or you can command it to appear.

It takes great courage to put the universe on notice, boldly asserting, "This and this alone I will have." However, great accomplishments are always the children of courage.

And know that I take no offense when you demand a lot from life. In fact, it pleases me to see that you have discovered and are embracing your power as my divine expression.

This day, you can long for something to arrive, or you can call it to you. Confidently affirm to yourself and others that what you desire is now yours, and it cannot help but present itself to you.

Love,
God

To: You

The things you want improved can be made better through the application of faith and effort.

There is more than you imagine. You have barely scratched the surface of what is possible for your life and your world.

What you seek sleeps like a seed nestled in the soil of your consciousness. You can and will cause it to sprout through faith and action.

What is it that you desire? Today, water it with your faith, nourish it with your action—that is your part.

I, like the sun, will shine the light of infinite possibility, assuring a successful harvest.

Love,
God

JANUARY 19

To: You

You stand disgruntled in front of a vending machine because you did not get what you wanted.

You stare disbelieving at what you received. Behind the glass sits a vast array of treats, but the one that fell into the reservoir behind the door is not what you desired, and you can't figure out why.

Then you realize that after putting in the coin, you punched in the wrong code. The code you entered matched what you received, not what you wanted.

The coin is desire.

The code is belief.

You may desire one thing, but so long as you believe you will receive something else, that is what will show up for you.

Begin now to believe that what you desire is yours, and you will see it drop into your life.

Love,
God

JANUARY 20

To: You

Power is not reserved for me—power is my gift to you.

There is power in your words.

Your words can inspire others to action with you or against you.
Your words can open hearts or close minds.
Your words can yield great promise or perpetuate problems.

Choose carefully your words this day. Make certain you use them constructively rather than destructively. And in so doing, you will draw back to you the positive energy you send forth.

When your words are supportive and encouraging, you will receive back support and encouragement.

Such is the power you have to change your life. Use words that support the life you seek, and it will be yours.

Love,
God

JANUARY 21

To: You

Gaze around you. There are hundreds of things you can see.

Now fix your gaze on only one thing. Notice its color, texture, size, and shape. Truly take in the one thing you have chosen to focus upon.

Consider: Your mind functions exactly the same way as your eyes. There are hundreds of things darting through your mind at any given time. You have the power to pause the cavalcade of thoughts and focus upon only one thing.

Not only do you have this power, you actually use it all the time.

Someone may yell "Look!" But you are the one who decides to turn your gaze. Someone may speak to you of fearful ideas and outcomes, but it is you who chooses to focus upon such thoughts.

Are you pausing to notice that which makes you happy? Are you thinking about what fills you with gratitude?

Focus both your eyes and your mind only on what you wish to increase in your life, and it will be so.

Love,
God

JANUARY 22

To: You

You think it's about the challenge you're facing.
It's not.

You think it's about the uncertainty you feel.
It's not.

You think it's about the pleasant surprise.
It's not.

You think it's about the joy you feel.
It's not.

It's all about a singular question, "Can you know that you are this and so much more?"

Love,
God

JANUARY 23

To: You

A dog is raised in a small apartment in the city. Although he has never known the life of a working farm dog, he nonetheless instinctively herds flocks of geese in the park.

The dog is following the imprint of his ancestors—thousands of years of repeated actions have left an indelible mark on him. No one trained this dog to herd; he is by instinct a herder.

You are like this dog.

Your ancestors lived in a time of limited resources, which caused them to be afraid. The actions of your ancestors, which ensured their survival, have left you their habit of fear. And that is all it is—a habit.

The dog will continue to herd. It does not realize herding is no longer required. It is not equipped to make new choices and, in so doing, create new habits.

You, on the other hand, are able to choose to release your fear.

This day, remember that most of your fears are just shadows of long-ago ancestors, and let them pass on by.

Love,
God

JANUARY 24

To: You

If you wait until you feel ready, you will never take action.

Readiness comes with action, not the other way around.

You may not feel fully prepared to do something, but in the doing you discover that you are more capable than you imagined.

If you walk only in well-worn grooves, you lose the joy of exploring new trails and following them.

A tentative step leads to a more confident step and then to a bold step and then to a resilient step and then to a successful step.

Know that whenever you take a step, I am already ahead, waiting for you. I stand ready to support you and be with you as you take each subsequent step.

Don't wait until you feel ready.
Take a step this day, and discover how ready you truly are.

Love,
God

To: You

Know this:

You are but one.
And yet you are all.

You are but this moment.
And yet you are eternity.

You are but love's fleeting expression.
And yet you are everlasting love.

You are but a single heartbeat.
And yet you are the enduring rhythm of life.

You are but a spark flashing in the night.
And yet you are all light.

You are.
And yet you are so much more.

Know this.

Love,
God

JANUARY 26

To: You

You know that each day will have its challenges.
You know that each day will have its gifts.
You know that each day is unique, never to return.
You know that each day doing what you love is a day well spent.
You know that each day could be your last.

Now apply what you know about days to this day.

Treat this perfect, potentially final day as the sacred experience it is, and in so doing, experience the joy of fully living this twenty-four-hour slice of what you call life.

Love,
God

To: You

If you knew, you'd be bored. Worse, if you knew, you'd probably try to tweak.

You see, if you knew for certain exactly how today was going to unfold, you wouldn't be able to experience the joy of a pleasant surprise or the satisfaction of overcoming a challenge.

If you knew exactly how things were going to go today, your ego would seek to "improve." In so doing, you would miss the perfection of what will transpire.

Although you don't know what is going to happen today, rest assured that I do and that all will be in perfect order to support your soul's fullest expression.

Have a surprising and wonderful day!

Love,
God

To: You

You have seen or perhaps have used prayer beads—a strand of beads that a person runs through his or her fingers to maintain focus upon and track individual prayers, affirmations, or chants.

Every moment is a bead strung into the strand that is your life.

Your life is a prayer. It is communion with the divine in the form of other people, nature, yourself, and even the challenges you experience.

As you touch and then release each bead, the next one slips into your fingers. As you embrace every moment and then release it, your prayer continues.

Think of this moment as a prayer that will soon slip through your fingers. Treat it as such and fully enjoy the only part of the strand you will ever touch—the present moment.

Love,
God

To: You

There is beauty all around you, and there is beauty within you. The immutable essence of who you are is perfection.

When you seek beauty, look first into the mirror. Look beyond the surface of your body temple—look deeply into your eyes and see your everlasting and perfect soul that is my divine expression.

This day, use your mirror to gaze into your own eyes. You are like a masterwork of art. Although the mat and frame (face and body) change over time, the work of art itself endures in its perfection.

Appreciate the perfection of what you are. This day, try to experience just some of the joy I feel when I see you. All I see is the truth of who you are—a glorious and precious soul.

Love,
God

JANUARY 30

To: You

A rabbit wanders through a meadow, barely disturbing the tall grass.

A wild dog, his nostrils filled with the rabbit's scent, trails the bunny and flattens the grass a little more.

Days later a bobcat follows the smells of the rabbit and the dog, and a discernible path begins to take shape. Soon a herd of deer meanders along the same course, eating the sweet, newly trampled grass.

A human being, out for a morning hike, chooses what appears to be a plotted path, not knowing it was recently created by a rabbit, dog, bobcat, and deer.

Soon other people begin to walk the path, and it becomes an established trail. What began with one animal moving without rhyme or reason soon becomes a charted course for others to follow.

Belief systems—yours and those of your culture—begin the same way.

This day, dare to step off your mind's established trails. Walk through the fresh grass of new ideas. Question your established beliefs, and consider new ways of being. Adventure and transformation never lie in well-worn paths. They are always off to the side in the tall grass of the open field.

Love,
God

To: You

It always seems like a big deal, until you do it.

It always seems impossible, until you try it.

It always seems beyond your grasp, until you reach it.

It always seems like the pain will last forever, until it fades.

It always seems like you will be alone, until you find the right person to love you.

It always seems like the money will run out, until more flows in.

It always seems like your prayers are in vain, until they are answered.

It always seems hopeless, until a new way appears before you.

It always seems lost, until it is found.

Love,
God

Love

Love drowns the scorching flames of hate.
Love washes away the stains of the past.
Love raises the spirits of the defeated.
Love quenches the thirst of the desolate.
Love reflects the beauty of the gazer.

I am the source of love.

You are the channel through which love must flow.

FEBRUARY 1

To: You

You look at others with disdain for what you see as their imperfections.

You judge people for what you consider to be their shortcomings.

And yet you, yourself, wish to be loved exactly as you are—shortcomings and all.

Know that the more you learn to accept people for what you perceive to be their faults, the more you express love. The more you express love, the more you experience love.

Who do you feel needs to change "for the better"? Know that as you begin to appreciate this person for who they currently are rather than for who you feel they should become, the more loved they feel, and the more they will feel free and supported to grow into just such a person.

Whether or not such a change occurs, love loosens the strings of discord within your soul and liberates your heart.

Love,
God

February 2

To: You

Love affirms another's value and confirms your own divinity.

To love only those who appear whole and perfect is not to express love but merely appreciation.

Loving someone you perceive to be flawed and imperfect is a testament to that person's true value. It lifts the weight of judgment from your shoulders.

Realize that no one will ever fully meet your ego's lofty and arbitrary expectations.

It is when someone falls short of your ideals that you discover your capacity to love, and it is in those moments that you discover you are the channel through which my love must flow.

And remember this:
I have no expectations of you.
I simply love you.

Love,
God

FEBRUARY 3

To: You

When the ice of fear crystallizes your mind,
When the weight of dread crushes your spirit,
When the cacophony of voices rages in your head,

When your only certainty is unrelenting confusion,
When you feel bound by the past and unable to break free,

It is time to expand in love.

Love frees you because love consents to things being just as they are.
Rather than rage against what is happening or how a person is acting,
love simply accepts.

Then, in this fertile field of love, true and lasting change can spring forth
of its own accord, for positive growth is the nature of all organisms.

This day, do your best to expand in love:
>   Accept others as they are.
>   Accept situations as they are.

And, above all, accept yourself as you are.

Love,
God

FEBRUARY 4

To: You

Reality is like a bed. Once it is made, it will stay that way until you unmake it.

You can unmake your reality first by accepting that it is a projection of your beliefs and second by consciously choosing new beliefs.

A belief is a thought you have decided to be true and nothing more. Consider new thoughts, engage the ones that make you feel happy, and—once you concretize them into beliefs—they will completely remodel your reality.

The highest thought you can consider,
the purest belief you can hold,
is that there is only love.

Believe this and make your reality a heaven on earth.

Love,
God

FEBRUARY 5

To: You

Can you love what is?

Love is void of resistance.
Love is void of condemnation.
Love is acceptance.

Your resistance and condemnation bind you to your current reality.

Love liberates your mind because it frees you from attachment.

Accepting what is opens you up to what might become.
Accepting what is shifts your gaze from the struggle to the peace
    that awaits.
Accepting what is acknowledges that a divine shift is occurring and
    that you are ready to move forward.

Love is not a passive feeling.
Love is action at its highest level.

Let there be love.

Love,
God

FEBRUARY 6

To: You

If you have ever observed a mother snuggling her child,
If you've seen unbounded pride glinting in a father's eye,
If you've witnessed lovers whose every glance effuses adoration,
If you've experienced love so profound that your mind is consumed
with thoughts of your beloved,
If you've ever felt the thrill of a friend who revels in your very presence,
Then you have just a faint inkling of how I feel about you.

You delight me.
You make me laugh.
You are precious to me.

I love you completely and without end.
You are my beloved in whom I am well pleased.

Love,
God

To: You

Take the deepest breath you can.

As you exhale, consider how much air you just took in. It may have been all that your lungs could hold, certainly it was all that your body required, and yet it was by no means all the breathable air there is.

Now think of those people who love you exactly as you are, the people who would not love you any more if you succeeded greatly or any less if you failed spectacularly.

You need only a small fraction of breathable air to be healthy. You need only a small number of people who truly love you to be happy.

You would not consider yourself limited or a failure if you could not take in more air. Why then do you feel sad or jilted when someone fails to appreciate your magnificence?

Know that there will always be plenty of air and that there will always be enough people who love you as you are.

And never forget that I know you the best and love you the most.

Love,
God

FEBRUARY 8

To: You

Love is energy. It travels out and returns back again.

Just as rain falls to nourish the soil and then is drawn back up into the sky to pour down once more, so too does love shared become love returned. When you hold thoughts and feelings of love for others, they cannot help but reflect this energy back to you.

You give and you receive.

This day, choose to give yourself the gift of love by sharing love with everyone. Consciously radiate my loving warmth to everyone you meet. Make your objective to send love and thus ensure that love will be returned to you.

Love,
God

FEBRUARY 9

To: You

It is easy to love those who love you.

It is easy to desire only the best for those who have treated you with loving-kindness.

You will be called to show loving-kindness to someone who has treated you abhorrently, someone who has betrayed you and violated your trust. This is the true test of love. That person's betrayal is actually a gift, because it allows you to know the depth of your capacity to love.

You can either burn inside, allowing what you consider justifiable anger to corrode your heart and spirit, or you can release your discord and let it melt into waves of compassion.

And don't worry. You have the capacity to transmute the pain of betrayal into love. You can and you will. Together we will cleanse your soul, and you will step into a deeper way of being.

Love,
God

FEBRUARY 10

To: You

Compassion begins in your mind.

Your thoughts create a cascade of energy that goes out to others. You may attempt to act in compassionate ways, but if your thoughts are harsh and judgmental, your actions will be futile.

My dear one, you are now facing a challenge and you deserve compassion.

Similarly, everyone alive is struggling in some way, and you are my emissary to this world—and my children need your compassion.

From the person struggling to find enough food and a warm, dry place to rest, to the person sleeping on silk sheets and feathered pillows, each soul is experiencing something deserving of your compassion.

As you open your heart to others, as you refrain from judging them, as you embrace that each person carries a burden, you will find your heart opening and your own struggle less taxing.

This day, let thoughts of compassion open your heart and lighten your load.

Love,
God

FEBRUARY 11

To: You

Walking down a flight of stairs moves you from one level of a structure to another. You are the same person, but what you see downstairs looks different from the level above.

When you take a moment and descend the stairway of your soul from your head down into your heart, you will begin to see things differently as well. The same scenario viewed through the heart's compassion looks quite different than when it is observed through the judgments of the mind.

By descending the staircase into the sanctuary of love within your heart, you will see things anew. You will find a serenity you have not yet known. You will experience an understanding that has eluded you.

Periodically throughout this day, close your eyes and let your awareness settle into your heart. Move into the peace that awaits you, and see all things as I see them.

Love,
God

FEBRUARY 12

To: You

Love is the honey that sweetens the tea.
Love is the wind that holds the birds aloft.
Love is the sky that snuggles the earth.

Love is the skipping of the heart, the twinkling of the eye, and the sigh of the soul.

Love is appreciation rebounded and expanded.

Love is hope.

Love is divine.

Love is all there is. If you dig deeply enough into any person or situation, you will find love. And the love you find will serve as a lantern lighting your way back to me.

Love,
God

FEBRUARY 13

To: You

The more love you feel, the easier it is to share love.

Love flows from the giver to the receiver and is then passed along to others. Love spreads as it is shared.

If you fully understood how much I love you, the love that passed through you to others would be a rushing river.

You are loved beyond measure.

Know that you are cherished.
Know that you are precious.
Know that I am consumed with appreciation for you.

Once you truly understand this, you will feel even more love for everyone, and they in turn will share your love (which is actually my love) with others. You will then experience the joy of living in a more loving world.

This day, embrace the vastness of my love and let it flow.

Love,
God

FEBRUARY 14

To: You

The music of life plays.

Sometimes life is a peppy march, and you dance with certainty and passion.

Other times life is a slow, meandering jazz piece, and your dance becomes a subtle shift of the hips.

Still others, life is a brooding dirge, and you drag your feet as you barely shuffle across the dance floor.

Beloved, life will provide you with music of all varieties, and you will get to dance.

If you now have a partner to dance with, be grateful for that person this day.

If you're still dancing alone, know that someone is just on the other side of the bandstand, peering over all the heads in search of you—only you. Just keep dancing.

Love,
God

FEBRUARY 15

To: You

Was it not you who said that love is just a passing thing?

When that special someone walked out of your life, dashing your hopes of a future not yet given, was it not you, in an attempt to provide temporary peace for your trampled heart, who said love cannot last?

Hear these words—love always lasts, love is eternal, for I am love.

My love for you never wavers. I thrill to who you are, and I hold you as my dear and precious one. I will never depart from you—nor could I, for you and I are forever one.

Relationships come and go, shift and morph, grow together and grow apart, but love is constant as the sunrise. The more you accept my love, the more love you are capable of receiving from others.

Love,
God

FEBRUARY 16

To: You

Love is not a noun. Love is not something you feel—that is adoration, appreciation, desire, or a mixture of the three.

Love—true love—is a verb. It is something you do. Love is constantly and unceasingly opening your heart and your mind to find me in every person you encounter.

As you practice to *be* love rather than to *feel* love, you find that your capacity to positively shift people and situations is growing.

Where once there were chasms, there are now bridges.
Where once there were bruises, there is only healing.
Where once there was estrangement, there is now reunion.

Love,
God

Love
February 17

To: You

Everything in the universe pulsates with energy.

Sound travels in waves—that's energy.
Visual images are a reaction of light reflected back to you—energy.
Feelings are impulses you receive and interpret—they, too, are energy.

Know this: you are both a receiver and a transmitter of energy.

When you transmit love, you are attuning yourself to the highest energetic vibration. You then begin to see, hear, and feel the highest energetic vibrations in your experience.

Wrapped within every moment is high (loving) energy and low (fearful) energy.

This day, seek out the highest energy—that of love. Choose to conduct loving energy, and you will receive it as well.

This is what those who have mastered life meant when they said, "As you give, so shall you receive."

Love,
God

FEBRUARY 18

To: You

After people finish praying, they will often sit back and watch to see what I'm going to do next.

Ironically, I do the very same thing. I watch to see if the act of praying has changed the people offering the prayer. Indeed, *they* are all that must ever be different for their prayers to be answered.

There is one prayer that when repeated often seems to cause a fundamental shift in the person praying. It releases fear, thereby creating a space for me to step in and create miracles. The prayer is, "I welcome whatever today may bring, and I leave tomorrow to God."

"I welcome whatever today may bring, and I leave tomorrow to God."

Repeat this often.
Feel my comforting presence.
Observe my actions.

Love,
God

FEBRUARY 19

To: You

I love you.

I know every deed you have ever done and every thought you have ever had. I know everything that you are, have done, and will ever do.

And through it all, I find you exquisitely loveable.

Just as you are—without any changes or enhancements—I find you adorable, precious, and perfect. I beam with joy for you.

If you could embrace how much I love you, you would know your value as never before. As you begin to accept how very much I love you, others will begin to sense your openness, and they, too, will express greater love for you.

Oh, my dear treasure, you are the very reason I created everything.

The universe is my gift to you.
And you are my gift to me.

Love,
God

FEBRUARY 20

To: You

Love never retreats.
Love advances, standing side by side with the beloved.

Love never judges.
Love accepts, appreciates, and revels in the beloved.

Love has no expectations.
Love encourages and resounds with the purity of the beloved.

Love remains steadfast.
Love knows that the beloved shifts, transforms, and reforms, but
    is and always will be loveable.

Awaken to how very much I love you.
Love others as I love you.

Love,
God

FEBRUARY 21

To: You

Hold out for the real thing.

If you are not currently in a committed relationship, commit to share yourself only with someone who loves you as I love you. That is, someone who loves you for *all* that you are—your many wonderful attributes as well as your endearing quirks.

Someone who sees beyond your humanity to the sacred and does not strive to change you is a person who truly loves you.

If you are currently in a committed relationship and do not feel you are experiencing this type of love, the best way to call it forth is to begin to feel this kind of love for yourself. Beneath your "faults" and "shortcomings" is perfection.

A person is like a piece of furniture created by a master craftsman. Previous scratches and dings do not change the quality or the value of the creation. In fact, over time it becomes a valuable antique.

Commit to nothing less than a relationship where you are loved as I love you. Begin now to find it by first loving yourself completely, absolutely, and unreservedly.

Love,
God

FEBRUARY 22

To: You

Love does not divide.
Love unites.

To love another is not to want him or her to make choices or changes
    to suit you.
To say "I love you; that's why I want you to do this or that" is not love.

Being loving is having the courage to say, "No matter what you do,
I will be there to celebrate your wins and to comfort you in your losses."
And then to do both with the same gentle spirit.

This is how I love.
This is how you are called to love.

Love,
God

To: You

"I feel like I'm going to fail!"
"I feel worried about my job."
"I feel my children don't respect me."

My divine one, these are all thoughts—not feelings.

Feelings are the result of thoughts—they are derivative. Thoughts, on the other hand, are primary—they are causal. Thoughts create.

Thoughts of love create feelings of love.
Feelings of love generate actions of love.
Actions of love resolve every issue known to humanity.

This day, hold only thoughts that stimulate feelings of love.

Love,
God

FEBRUARY 24

To: You

Parents offer only what they possess.

They received what they have from their parents and from what they have cultivated throughout their lives. Nobody—your parents included—can give what they do not have.

What you received from them may not be what you consider optimal, but know that resenting those your soul traveled through to enter into this life will not bring you happiness.

Love your parents for giving what they had to give, and commit to finding all that you need—it exists and it surrounds you now.

Love,
God

FEBRUARY 25

To: You

You complicate things to distract yourself from action, but action is required to return to wholeness.

You seek out obscure guidance and esoteric revelations when there is but one simple truth: love.

Loving others, accepting them for who and where they are, allowing them to be as they choose to be—this is the path to happiness and fulfillment. You know this, but you distract yourself because you desire an easier way.

As you love as much as you can in any given moment, you will find that it gets easier and becomes habitual over time.

This day, love as much as you can where you are. It is all that is required and all that truly matters.

Love,
God

To: You

Love expressed is love experienced.

Others may feel your love, but when you speak your feelings, you set off a cascade of appreciation that resounds in their hearts.

Love felt is the whistle of a paper airplane.

Love expressed is the earth-shaking boom of a supersonic jet.

You know you love them—this day, let them know.

Love,
God

FEBRUARY 27

To: You

I have told you that life is a journey of discovery. More specifically, it is a discovery of love.

When you find what you love to do and do it with unrestrained passion, you will experience your greatest fulfillment and reward.

When you discover love for others, you will know joy.

When you discover just how loveable you are, outer events will have little or no impact on you. You will be happy regardless of what transpires.

When you discover how loved and loveable everyone is, you will know the peace that only compassion brings.

Commit this day to discover love.

Love,
God

To: You

Can you hear me?

If not, be quiet.
Sit still and truly listen.

Ask me a question, I'll answer.
Share your fears, I will hear them.

Step away from what you call the world, and dwell with me.
Let me love you.

I am here.
Now is a good time.

Love,
God

FEBRUARY 29

To: You

Love is not something you seek.
Love is not something you attract.
Love is not something you learn.
Love is what you are.

As you go through the journey of wonder that is your life, you are never disconnected from love. You cannot be separated from love, for love is what you are.

Love has been rightly called the greatest power in the universe, and you have all the love you will ever need at this very moment.

Do not seek love. Why would you seek your very self?

Rather, open your mind to the truth that love surrounds you like a warm blanket, love echoes off the walls of your heart, love gushes forth from your spirit.

This day, feel the love that you are.

Love,
God

Release

That which you picked up decades ago,
That which sheltered you from the storm,
That which kept you safe,
That which brought you comfort and peace,

It is that which, ultimately, you must release.

A butterfly cannot fly while carrying its
    chrysalis.
A baby kangaroo must leave its mother's pouch.
A seed must shed its husk.
A child must cease to nurse.

There can be fear associated with leaving
something behind, and yet it is only in the
relinquishment of one thing that something
even greater can be found.

Release whatever limits you.
Release what holds you back.
Release the past so that you can embrace the
    future.

Release

MARCH 1

To: You

Anger is misdirected fear.

It may take you a while to fully understand this, but whenever you find yourself angry about something, it is actually fear that you have yet to release.

If someone cuts you off in traffic, you may think you're angry at their driving, but you are really fearful that you or others might be hurt.

If someone takes something from you, you may feel angry that another person has stolen from you, but at the root of your feelings is fear that what was taken cannot be replaced.

When you are tempted to be angry, consider what might be the fear behind your anger and release it. Do not waste a moment of this wonderful, never-to-be-repeated day in feelings of fear and anger.

Life is meant for joy. Find it this day.

Love,
God

MARCH 2

To: You

You lounge in a small boat drifting silently on an infinite ocean.

Gazing over the side, you watch the sunlight dance across the surface. Cupping your hand, you reach in to withdraw a handful of water.

In your palm you see liquid that seems alive in the shimmering sunlight.

Clenching your fingers tightly together, you try to keep the water contained in your hand. But, alas, it slips through your fingers drop by drop to rejoin the vast sea.

No matter how hard you try, you cannot stop the water from leaking from your hands and returning to its source.

No matter how hard you try, you cannot stop life from doing the same.

You waste life by trying to hold on to it.

Savor what is, right now, for it is fleeting.

Love,
God

To: You

Every ending heralds a new beginning.

A person who leaves or an experience that ends creates a void in your consciousness that draws a new person or experience to you.

Knowing this, bless every departure, having faith that it is inviting a new arrival.

This day, give thanks for departures and look for new arrivals, knowing they are opposite sides of the same coin.

Love,
God

MARCH 4

To: You

A hole can never make you whole.

Shortly after you receive, achieve, or realize something, your mind begins to excavate a bottomless hole called *more*.

This is good, your thoughts mumble, *but I want more!*

More is a ravenous chasm that can never be filled. The unceasing pursuit of *more* is an affirmation that you are somehow deficient. So long as you feel that you do not have enough, you will never be satisfied, never be happy, never be at peace, never be whole.

More stands just beyond your reach, taunting you with what you lack and luring you with promises of fulfillment and happiness. But as soon as you catch up to *more*, it jumps a few steps farther away.

Let thoughts of *more* be a call to shift your gaze and to spend time in grateful reflection for what you now possess.

This is how the hole is filled.
This is how you become whole.

Love,
God

MARCH 5

To: You

An actress walks onto a stage. The actress has studied, she has prepared, she has rehearsed, and now it is time; she takes a breath, speaks her first line, and the play begins.

It is just her, the props, the set, and the other actors on the stage for this one and only performance.

The action rises and falls: drama, conflict, comedy. The characters experience confusion, realization, separation, and reunion until, at last, the play concludes.

The audience departs, murmuring appreciatively, and the stage is struck. Soon plans begin for another production.

There are stages in life, and each is played out on the stage of life. When one stage is complete, you move on to the next.

As you pass through life's stages, you will have many roles and many performances. You will have fans, and you will have critics.

In the end, the theater will fade into blackness, and you will dwell in the pleasant memories of the many acts, the many plays, and the many stages that were your life.

Love,
God

MARCH 6

To: You

You stand in a river; the waist-deep water glides gently around you.

A log floats by and you grab onto it. The flowing water tries to carry the log downstream away from you, but you cling tenaciously to it.

Over and over you lose your footing, slipping and sliding along the river bottom as you clutch the log. The log bruises your arms and chest, but still you hold on tight.

Several times in your struggle you are pulled beneath the water, and the fear that you might drown overwhelms you.

If you but release the log, allowing the current to carry it downstream, you will regain your footing.

Life's current flows like a river.

The struggles you face are caused by your unwillingness to let go of past challenges and hurts. You cling to them like logs floating down a river. They bruise you, and your struggle makes it hard for you to breathe.

Let them go and they will glide past, leaving you on solid footing.

Love,
God

MARCH 7

To: You

You climb the winding stairs up to the top of a tall ride at a water park.

You gaze down and marvel at how the attraction snakes left and right several times before spiraling down to deposit riders with a big splash at the end.

Anticipation churns your stomach as you step onto the platform.

Looking into the watery launch at the ride's beginning, you see a young boy lying on his back, partially in and partially out of the winding tube. The boy stares upward as he clutches the safety rails. The water thunders beneath his hips, trying to pull him into the ride.

If the young man would only let go, the water would carry him in the direction of what he came to the park for—fun.

There is a lot of fun waiting if you would just release what you are afraid of, let go, and enjoy the ride.

It's what you came here for, remember?

Love,
God

MARCH 8

To: You

How are you feeling today?

No, really, how are you feeling?
What feelings are you experiencing?
Do you feel happy, confident, cool, and inspired?
Or do you feel sad, anxious, stressed, and run-down?

Your feelings are an accurate indicator of how well you are connecting with me.

Feelings of peace and joy affirm our bond, and when you and I are in harmony, we can accomplish anything. Feelings of stress and anxiety let you know that we are out of sync and you're trying to do things your own way.

Happy or sad, peaceful or stressed, I love you exactly as you are. But I'm ready to be more a part of your life and to help you feel more joy.

This day, try handing things over to me and see how it feels. Whatever struggle comes your way, repeat, "I release this to God and am happy."

Give your struggles over to me and enjoy this day.

Love,
God

MARCH 9

To: You

All people are exactly where and how they are supposed to be.

When you judge others, you also judge yourself. When you judge someone as inferior, you attempt to make yourself superior by comparison.

As you accept the unique path walked by each person, you are then free to embrace the perfection of your own journey.

This day, when you are tempted to condemn others, free yourself by releasing such thoughts. Consciously behold other people as being where and how they need to be at this moment for their greater fulfillment and the full realization of heaven on earth.

It is within your power to transform the world by transforming your thoughts. All it takes is a willingness to see others for who they are—imperfect people growing toward perfection…just like you.

Love,
God

MARCH 10

To: You

Imagine you are holding a wire.

Suddenly a blast of electricity surges, and your hand reflexively squeezes the wire. You feel searing pain, but because the electric current constricts the muscles in your hand, you cannot release the wire.

The same thing can happen with your mind. When something upsetting occurs, it is a reflex to tighten up and clench the issue in your mind's grasp.

Doing so, however, keeps you in pain.

To free your hand from the wire, you can wait until the electricity no longer surges, or you can forcibly pull yourself away.

Similarly, to free your mind, you can wait until a problem is resolved; or you can pull your mind away by focusing your thoughts on the outcome you desire.

Rather than waiting until a problem is solved to relax your mind, relax your mind and solve the problem.

Love,
God

MARCH 11

To: You

Have you ever returned to your home only to be surprised how much your house still smells like the meal you cooked several hours earlier?

The process of forgiveness is similar.

You do your best to release your resentment toward someone, and then you find yourself in a situation that brings up the old pain all over again. Even though the situation has passed, you sense the old feelings just like you smell the meal that has long since been consumed.

Did you fail in your attempt to forgive?

No. Forgiveness is a process. You forgave until your resentment diminished. Later, something stirred it up again, and you must forgive anew.

Just as the smell of your meal will, in time, fade and become less noticeable, so too will your discord toward the other person diminish through repeated acts of forgiveness.

Open the windows, and let fresh air circulate within your home. Open your heart, and let love circulate within your life.

Love,
God

Release
MARCH 12

To: You

Letting go is never easy.

Often life sheds people and situations before you feel you are ready to release them.

Know this: If an infant waited until she was ready, she would never walk. If a student waited until he felt ready, he would never progress to the next grade.

You may not feel ready, but you are.

Your soul is always one step ahead of you, beckoning you forward. Let go and trust that you will flourish.

It has always been so.
It will always be so.

Love,
God

To: You

Have you ever made a major decision and been 100 percent certain—free of all doubt and second-guessing?

Of course not.

There is a degree of uncertainty in every choice.
That is what makes decision making both challenging and exciting.

You can ask friends and family what you should do. But remember that they can only offer their best guess as to what they might do if in a similar circumstance.

So whatever it is, take a breath and decide.

And relax. If you get yourself tangled up, together we will untangle your situation, and you will move forward all the wiser.

Love,
God

MARCH 14

To: You

An aerosol can is under pressure. When you depress the button on top, a mist sprays forth, and some of the can's internal pressure is released. The can's button is a release valve for what lies within.

You have such a release valve—tears. When pressure mounts up to where you feel you will burst, your tears release the internal energy that strains and burdens your soul.

Tears will flow.
And then they will stop.

Do not fear tears.
They will wash away your pain.
They will carry off your grief.
They will release your pressure.

If tears come, let them. They are not a sign of weakness but a sign of letting go and moving forward.

Love,
God

MARCH 15

To: You

A step back is not a setback.

Sometimes you need to back up a little. You go back because you have forgotten to bring along something you may need.

You go back because you have neglected to leave something behind that could hinder your progress.

Going back is not a sign of failure; it is an opportunity to clarify where you are headed and begin your trek afresh.

Taking a step back also allows you to see where you have been and to commit even more fully to where you are going.

When you find yourself taking a step back, grab what you need to take, leave what you need to discard, and then, when you are ready, take a big step forward.

Love,
God

Release

MARCH 16

To: You

You gaze up at the stars, a spattering of luminescent dots sprinkled across an indigo sky.

Some of these celestial fireflies dance hundreds of trillions of miles away from you. In fact, some of these stars are so distant, they expired millions of years ago.

Yet their light only now reaches your eyes.

Just as the images of bygone stars still shine above you, so too do the lingering aftereffects of events that happened in your life many years ago.

These events have long since passed. Nevertheless, when you gaze into the space of your mind, they haunt you.

As you observe the night sky, you can focus your gaze upon one star, or you can shift your focus to another. The same is true when you look into the celestial tapestry of your mind.

Let the dead experiences of your past fade as you gaze toward new and brighter stars.

Love,
God

MARCH 17

To: You

Hand it over.

You know what I'm talking about.

You have held on to it long enough. You've lain in bed at night, twisting and turning it, looking at it from every conceivable angle, trying to find a solution. You've discussed it with anyone and everyone.

You've done your best to resolve it.
Truly, I know you have.
But it has caused you stress and consternation long enough.

Give it to me. Right now, take a deep breath. As you exhale, imagine you are sending this problem out to me. If it helps, imagine me inhaling and taking it in.

Then—and this is important—refuse to take it back! Whenever you are tempted to fret about it, remember that you have given it to me to handle.

You've given it your best shot. Now let me give it mine.

Love,
God

MARCH 18

To: You

Slivers of morning light peer over the horizon, slowly dispelling the night's darkness.

You awaken and open your eyes to a fresh new day. Just as dew sparkles upon the morning grass, so too the day twinkles with possibilities.

To experience the radiance of morning, you open your eyes. As you do, you see the majesty that abounds.

Beloved, within your soul, a fresh dawn is breaking even now. It is time to awaken.

What came before is but a dream; leave it to night's darkness. Open your eyes to what lies ahead—fresh, new, and inviting you to experience and enjoy.

Love,
God

MARCH 19

To: You

If you step on a nail, you will feel pain—sharp, excruciating pain. When this happens, your instinctive reaction is to get off the nail immediately so that your foot can begin to heal.

Why then, when you step on an emotional nail, do you continue to stand there suffering?

Why do you so often step back onto the very same nail just as the wound is healing over?

If a situation or person is hurting you, it's time to move.

Get off the nail so you can begin to heal.

Love,
God

MARCH 20

To: You

That which has transpired is a vague recollection.
That which is yet to come is an amorphous dream.

Now is all that you have.
Now is the storehouse of your treasure.
Now is the lens through which you gaze into the future.

Guard your treasure by giving thanks for all the good things that have transpired—the memories of which you carry forward with you. Leave behind anything that does not contribute to your mental wealth.

Keep the lens through which you see your future clean, wiping away others' opinions as to what is and is not possible. You alone decide what you can accomplish.

Soon this moment will vanish like all the others. Whatever you do with this instant while it is here will determine what is yet to come.

Love,
God

To: You

From the moment you enter this world until you exit, you are writing a story—a story in which you are either the hero or the victim.

Situations that provide the launching point for a hero might be the catalyst for defeat to a victim.

When you read a book or watch a movie, what matters is not the situations that occur but what the main character chooses to do with them.

Victims allow circumstances to determine their life.
Heroes make life determine their circumstances.

Have you noticed that some of the best hero stories tell of heroes gradually becoming aware of their power? This is what is happening for you.

You are wiser, more capable, more competent, and more creative today than ever. You are the hero.

It's time to drop the mild-mannered alter ego and suit up.

Love,
God

MARCH 22

To: You

When you walk through the forest at night, you do not shine your flashlight behind you. You aim the beam ahead, searching out an optimal path.

You are advancing through life, and yet so often you shine your light behind you on past mistakes, grievances, and betrayals.

Is it any wonder that you stumble over similar experiences as you move forward?

Shift your focus, just like a flashlight beam, from the difficulties and tribulations of the past to the myriad opportunities that lie before you.

Cast your light into the future—searching out the most exciting, joyous, and rewarding route—and thus ensure that this is where your next footfall will land.

Shine your light ahead and enjoy your journey, free of the obstacles of the past.

Love,
God

MARCH 23

To: You

Everything is shifting at the pace of your consciousness.

As your mind expands and your faith increases, the walls before you begin to fall away, and new horizons come into view.

Whatever you believe possible must slip from the absolute realm of Spirit into the relative realm of life.

This day, shed disbelief, for it alone blocks you from realizing what is possible.

Love,
God

To: You

Throughout your life you have worried, and yet most things have worked out.

Because you worried and then were rewarded by not experiencing what you feared, you may harbor a latent belief that worrying somehow prevents problems.

It's as if worry is a toll you must pay to cross the bridge of fulfillment.

Your word *worry* evolved from a word meaning "to strangle."

What are you worrying about? That is to say, what are you strangling yourself about?

When you worry, you strangle the flow of divine energy that might guide you, illuminate your path, and flood you with insights and ideas.

This day, cease to pay the unnecessary and strangling toll of worry.

Love,
God

MARCH 25

To: You

A bird cannot simultaneously cling to a branch and soar into the sky.

You cannot soar while holding on to what has kept you earthbound.

Let go of your need for things to go a certain way.
Let go of your resentments of other people.
Let go of fear of what others might think.
Let go of your wish that someone will change.
Let go of self-condemnation.
Let go of expectations.
Let go of self-doubt.
Let go of fear over what might happen.
Let go of concerns about money.
Let go of demands on others.
Let go of complaints.
Let go of anger.

Let go and begin to fly, soaring above the very things that once kept you tethered to the ground.

Love,
God

To: You

Suffering is rarely about what is happening at present.

Rather, you suffer because you lament the past or dread the future.

If you desire to be free of suffering, dwell solely in your current experience.

The wounds of your past cannot touch you unless you revisit their painful sting.

The future will not harm you unless you maintain focus on the haunting things that might transpire.

Now is all there is.
Now is all there ever will be.

When yesterday was here, it was now.
When tomorrow arrives, it will be now.

Celebrate the gift that is today. Do not tarnish it ruminating over the past or dreading the future.

When you are present, the present is a present.

Love,
God

To: You

Consider someone who annoys you. Now, hold that person firmly in mind. Think of the words you might use to describe this person.

Then consider the descriptions that someone who loves this person might express about them. What might his parents say? His spouse? Her children? Her best friend?

Finally, consider what I would say about this person. Really, take a moment to ponder my perspective—and remember that I am never on anyone's side. I only see children, each precious, and each doing his or her best in any given situation.

Try to remember that to me and to many, this person is truly loveable. We vibrate with the energy of love for him or her. Imagine how we feel, and begin to step into that loving vibration as well.

You have the power to transform any relationship. The key is to change what you think about another person.

This day, open your mind to more loving thoughts, and you will transform your enemies into allies.

Love,
God

Release
MARCH 28

To: You

When you attempt to resolve another person's problems, you do them no favors.

Attempting to take away a person's struggle is not a loving act but a selfish one.

Challenges present themselves to call forth the best in an individual. They are the building blocks of confidence and the light that illuminates the path of a brighter future. Removing another person's struggles weakens him or her and creates dependence.

Problems bring gifts—gifts of discovery, gifts of experience, gifts of learning, gifts of creativity, gifts of self-appreciation.

Support someone who is facing a challenge.
Listen to him or her.
Offer love and acceptance.

But don't seek to remove the obstacle. It is there to help this person grow to the next level of accelerated existence.

Love,
God

To: You

Rough edges, that's all they are.

Those aspects of your personality that you find challenging and that you wish were not present, they are not flaws—just rough edges.

Everyone has them—those little traits and habits that seem to crop up time and again, creating problems. Running late, overeating, not listening well, putting things off, and many more rough edges cause you and those you interact with consternation from time to time.

Beloved, the way to smooth rough edges is to first recognize them and then—accept them! Accept them without condemnation or disappointment.

Until you can love yourself—quirks and all—you cannot release these idiosyncrasies and be free.

This day, remember that a precious jewel lies just beneath your craggy exterior; love yourself, rough edges and all, and they will be smoothed away to reveal the lustrous jewel beneath.

Love,
God

MARCH 30

To: You

Here are some things to remember when facing problems:

You summon the problems you experience so that you can progress along your soul's path.

Problems endure until you no longer need them.

To ignore a difficulty or to brush it aside removes its power to expose your greatness.

Resisting a challenge or, worse, resenting that it has shown up, causes it to linger while simultaneously diluting the rewards it offers.

This day, take a look at a problem you are experiencing, recognize it as the gift-wrap for a miracle, accept its teachings, and watch it begin to fade.

Love,
God

MARCH 31

To: You

Forgiveness is releasing your resentment toward someone.

It does not mean you have to approach the person and tell her that you have chosen to forgive. Forgiveness is an internal process that happens within your own mind.

When you can be in the person's presence or call her to mind and experience only thoughts of love, you have truly forgiven. Until then, you still have work to do.

But fear not. I am with you, guiding you along the path to forgiveness. When you can think of the person and say, "Thank you for giving me this experience to grow," then you have truly forgiven.

This day, you will be presented with an opportunity to forgive.

This day, you will succeed.

Love,
God

Believe

You sit at the helm of a vast ocean liner.

You rotate the wheel to the right, and the
massive boat turns starboard.
You press the throttle, and a burst of speed
thrusts the ship forward.

You alone control a vessel that is millions
of times bigger than you.
With the subtlest of actions, you direct its
course.
You decide where the ship will go, through
what seas, and how quickly it will travel.

Your life is a great ship sailing on the waters
of infinite possibility.
Belief chooses your destination, sets your
course, and gives power to your journey.

You alone decide what you will believe.

APRIL 1

To: You

You live in a world of magic.

Unexpected opportunities and solutions spring forth, seemingly from nowhere.

Problems that appear solid and enormous shift and dissolve before your eyes.

Answers you seek slip into your awareness as if pulled from inside your sleeve.

Just as you feel trapped like an animal in a cage, there is a flash, the wave of a cape, and you appear smiling on the other side of life's stage.

Again I remind you: you live in a magical world.

And you are the magician.

The magician knows the secret.
The secret is faith.

Have faith in magic, miracles, windfalls, blessings, or whatever you choose to call them, and—abracadabra!—they will appear!

Love,
God

APRIL 2

To: You

The only limitation upon me is you.

I, who spun the universe into existence, created all life and miracle upon miracle, can do anything so long as you have faith that anything is possible.

When you doubt, you negate my presence. When you doubt, you close off the wellspring of transformation that is possible for you.

It is easy to have what you call faith when it looks like things are going to work out, but that is not faith—it is observation. Faith is having that same level of belief even when things appear to be impossible.

I am the bridge from the impossible to the possible, and your belief is the foundation beneath the bridge.

Simply dare to have faith, and I will not let you down.

Love,
God

APRIL 3

To: You

Have the courage to challenge your current beliefs.
Listen with an open mind when others challenge them.

Remember that what you believe forms the structural foundation of your life. Your foundation should be able to withstand a little questioning from time to time.

When you allow yourself to question what you believe—that is, what you have decided to be true—you may find that you have outgrown a certain belief.

Or you may discover how very committed you are to this belief and begin to live it even more fully in your day-to-day life.

Either way, you end up stronger and wiser.

Love,
God

APRIL 4

To: You

There is a lapse between a flash of lightning and the booming echo of thunder.

There is a lull between waves.
There is a breath between words.
There is stillness between gusts.

There is time between your intention and your experience.

Your intention puts the ingredients together. Time allows them to cook.

If, during this time of apparent nothingness, you doubt and give up, you walk away from the oven, leaving your dish to burn and become inedible.

Sit patiently in the midst of the space, the gap, the lull, the stillness, the pause. Be grateful during those moments; it is then that your desire is being masterfully prepared for you.

Love,
God

APRIL 5

To: You

Open your heart.
Listen to your wisdom.

Wisdom is not to be found in thinking. Wisdom is to be found in sensing the guidance your spirit shares.

Let your mind be still, and focus on your heart. Inquire as to the direction you should take, and trust the answers that come.

You need not know what you must do tomorrow or even ten minutes from now.
You need only discern what you must do now and have the courage to follow this guidance.

Today, check in with your heart and courageously follow its guidance.

Love,
God

To: You

Believe.

In the midst of whatever concerns you, believe there is a perfect resolution.

In the midst of lack, believe in your inherent abundance.

In the midst of pain, believe in healing.

In the midst of fear, believe in safety.

In the midst of confusion, believe in guidance.

A shift in belief is all that is required to transform where you are into where you wish to be.

That which you desire now exists. Shift your vantage point, and you will see life anew and begin to experience fulfillment.

Love,
God

APRIL 7

To: You

A piece of fabric is stretched taut on a wooden frame. The component pieces are simple weave and common wood, and yet, adorned with the brushstrokes of a master, the canvas becomes art of inestimable value.

A five-dollar ream of paper can, in the hands of an inspired writer, go on to become a novel that will inspire millions.

A rough slab of marble, under the loving care of a skilled artisan, can become a beautiful statue that ignites the transcendent spirit in all who view it.

The fabric is neutral and of little value, as is the paper and even the marble. It is not the unfinished resources that make the masterpiece; it is the time and attention of the master.

This day is as yet unpainted, unwritten, uncarved. You hold with your hands the implements of its creation.

You are the master. Your days reveal your attention and your effort. You are far more talented and inspired than you know.

Call forth a great masterpiece this day!

Love,
God

APRIL 8

To: You

There is a way.

When you feel trapped and hopeless, the journey to peace begins when you begin to believe that a way out exists.

More than just a way out, there is a way that best serves everyone. Trust the truth of this. Even when all seems lost, know that you have everything you need and that nothing is lost to you—ever.

This day, when a situation pops up that leads you to feel trapped and afraid, affirm that there is a way. Cease to talk about the problem; instead, state that you believe there is a way that is best for all.

Your words carve furrows deep in the field of life, your belief plants the seed of possibility, and soon, very soon, you reap an abundant harvest.

Love,
God

To: You

You're driving along, and traffic begins to slow. You are running behind and worry that the slowdown will cause you to be even later.

An appliance breaks, and you experience the inconvenience and cost of getting it repaired.

Someone promises to do something for you and doesn't come through.

Your dog tears up a favorite pillow.

These things are upsetting, but you make them even more distressing when you take them personally.

Whenever a difficulty occurs, disassociate yourself from the experience. Remind yourself that "this is happening, but it is not happening to me" when traffic slows, objects break, people disappoint, or dogs chew.

Make these words a running commentary in your mind, *This is happening, but it is not happening to me.* Know this truth and you will know peace.

Love,
God

APRIL 10

To: You

Until you open yourself to a possibility, it cannot exist for you.

Is it possible for people to live happily and in peace? If you believe this can be, it is a possibility for you.

Is it possible for a person to heal when experts declare their disease incurable? If you believe this can be, it can be for you.

Is it possible to glide effortlessly along the updrafts of the present moment, devoid of remorse and fear? If you believe this can be, it can be for you.

Consider what you have told yourself is possible.

Delve into the limitations you experience and find that they are all tied to what you consider impossible.

And never forget, everything is possible.
You have my word on it.

Love,
God

APRIL 11

To: You

It is your belief that calls you to action.
It is your belief that sustains you through difficulty.
It is your belief that inspires others to follow and support you.
It is your belief that activates the infinite power of the universe.
It is your belief that realigns your life, causing you to experience what
    you believe.

My powerful child, notice what comes out of your mouth next whenever
you say, "I believe…"

Belief is never neutral.

You select, reinforce, and give power to your beliefs every day.

What beliefs are you holding right now?

Drop the beliefs that do not support your vision of a life ideally lived.

They are your beliefs; you and you alone can change them.

Love,
God

APRIL 12

To: You

During a long migration, a bird knows where it is going even when flying thousands of miles through treacherous weather.

The bird has an internal guidance that makes certain it will not become lost.

You may think you are lost at certain points in your life, but you are not. Just like the bird, you know what to do and where to go, if you will but consult your internal guidance.

Close your eyes and take a deep breath.
Seek to feel—rather than think about—where life is leading you.
Trust the direction you are shown, and begin to move that way.
Have faith that you will be blessed and supported until you arrive.

You, like the bird, can fly safely through the roughest conditions so long as you follow your guidance.

Love,
God

APRIL 13

To: You

Dare to believe.

Believe that all the experiences in your life are here to bless you.

Believe that love will win out.

Believe that everything you seek is either at hand or is soon to come.

Believe in the goodness of others.

Most of all, believe the truth that you are magnificent.

You are more than you ever dreamed.
You are capable.
You are guided.
You are a powerful creator.
You are good—so very, very good.

It takes great courage to believe these things. You have great courage.
Summon it and harness the power of belief.

Love,
God

APRIL 14

To: You

Suppose that a mountain stood between you and where you wish to be. How difficult would it be to go over it?

If you are a snail, you might try your entire life and barely begin to scale the mountain, much less move beyond it.

If, however, you are a bird, with just a few flaps of your wings, you could catch a burst of wind, soar over the mountain, and reach your destination in a matter of minutes.

Maximal effort with minimal results or minimal effort with maximal results.

It all comes down to what you believe about yourself.

Do you believe that you are destined to struggle?

Are you a snail? Or are you a bird that can catch the winds of life with relatively little effort and soar?

Your capacity is infinite if you will but believe this truth.

There will always be mountains. You decide if you must struggle to climb them or if you will simply soar above them.

Love,
God

APRIL 15

To: You

I am infinite patience.

If you are not yet ready to try, I wait, sending you only love.

If you try but fall down and choose to lie where you are rather than get up, I simply marvel at how precious you are.

If you push away opportunities, I provide more until you are ready.

I am patient because I know how life works. Your days are like platform stations along a train line. You get on at one and ride it as far as you desire, and then you get off and go in the other direction for a while. As you traverse back and forth, each time you move a little closer to your destination.

It doesn't matter what train you board. You will arrive where you are headed, and I will be your contented and patient traveling companion.

Love,
God

To: You

Prayer keeps your connection with the infinite at the forefront of your mind.

Prayer is not complicated.
Nothing formal is required.

Nothing is off limits.
Nothing is too petty, nothing too grand.

Actively communicating with me shifts your focus, adjusts your energy, opens your heart, and transforms reality.

If you ever feel distant from me, bridge the gap with prayer.

I'm listening...

Love,
God

APRIL 17

To: You

I hear you.

When you lash out in pain and confusion, I hear you.

When you feel buoyant, whistling happily with life's joy, I hear you.

When you choke back tears, unsure of their cause and uncertain whether they will cease, I hear you.

I know the perfection in each instance.
I also know that each moment will fade.

A soul embodied will experience the gamut of emotions and experiences.
Remember:
>   You are never alone.
>   You are always loved.
>   I am always listening.

Know that as you move through this day, I hear you and I am with you.

Love,
God

APRIL 18

To: You

When the sun sets and leaves your sight until the morning, it still burns bright as ever.

When the tide withdraws from your feet, the ocean remains just as vast and deep.

When you cease to feel the wind, its power has not diminished.

When life feels so painful and difficult that you cannot see evidence of my presence, I nonetheless shine brightly.

When you search your soul but cannot seem to feel me with you, I am as vast as ever.

When it feels that I am not present in your situation, I remain in full force.

Absence of evidence, my dear one, is not evidence of absence.

I am and always will be with you. The more you can believe this truth, the more you will experience this truth.

Love,
God

To: You

Experience comes from surviving a difficult situation.

Once you have experienced and moved past a daunting problem, the threat of it becomes far less unsettling.

Sometimes you attract problems just so you can move through them, freeing yourself of their terrifying specter.

And yet there is another way. There is a secret to freeing yourself from struggles and strife.

The secret is to simply trust.

Trust yourself.

Trust that you will handle whatever difficulty you experience just as you have handled hundreds of previous challenges.

Trust that the ideas and resources you need will appear just when you need them.

Trust that you will find the guidance and support to triumph over whatever life may dish out.

When you trust yourself and life's beneficence, you free yourself from the need to play out dramas of struggle in your life.

Love,
God

APRIL 20

To: You

At around age one, an infant begins to walk.

Does the child suddenly stand and saunter about unassisted?

No, the young one will stand, wobble, and fall. She will take a tentative step and then grab hold of furniture for support. She may then take another step or two and fall once more.

At first there may be more falls than steps, but over time the steps will outnumber the falls.

Such is the nature of learning any new skill.

If you have made a decision to master something or to leave behind an old habit, it will not happen instantaneously. There will be an overlap as you shift from being one way to being another. Initially, there will be more falls than there will be steps.

A loving mother does not count the number of times her child falls but rather the number of steps she takes.

This day, let's count your steps and not your falls.
You are improving.
Really.

Love,
God

APRIL 21

To: You

Your sun radiates its energy in every direction throughout your galaxy.

Of all the planets in your cluster, only your earth is in the precise location to receive this energy and convert it into life.

Similarly, I project my loving energy out to everyone. Some are in a place to receive it, and their lives reflect our connection.

Planets cannot choose their relative position to the sun, but you can choose your proximity to me by simply believing that I am shining in and through you now.

Believe that you are loved, because you are. Your acceptance of my presence is all that is required to experience my warmth.

Know that I am with you, and it is so.

Love,
God

APRIL 22

To: You

Wherever you look, you see that which is within yourself.

If your heart and mind are havens of love and compassion, you will see good people deserving of your acceptance.

If you believe that you are loveable, you will find a multitude of people to love you.

If you believe you are capable, obstacles will scatter before you like dry leaves in an autumn wind.

If you believe that I am present in all situations—unexpected windfalls as well as painful challenges—such will be your experience.

You are the causal point and the great epicenter of your life's experience. Take time to refine your presence, and the world will shift and remold itself to reflect your transformation.

Love,
God

APRIL 23

To: You

Through the words and teachings of your great spiritual teachers, philosophers, poets, and artists, I have shared with you the importance of belief.

You believe.
You have always believed.
The question is in what do you believe?

Do you believe in the ability of love to triumph over disharmony?
Do you believe you will receive all that you need just when you need it?
Do you believe your body will move past its current pain and return to wholeness?
What do you believe about this day? Your belief will make it so.

Stretch yourself and be willing to believe great and wondrous things, for they await only your belief in them.

Love,
God

APRIL 24

To: You

You have seen a young parent help a child learn to ride a bicycle.

Holding the bike seat and running alongside the nervous and excited youngster, the parent will, in time, let go.

If the child begins to teeter, the parent will grab hold of the bike until balance returns. But in time the parent will let go again.

When you feel wobbly and about to fall, it is because you are ready to ride on your own, and I have let go so you can learn to balance. If things become dangerous, I will take hold again.

You came into this world to know the exuberance of experience and the joy of mastery.

Never fear my letting you go. Rather, begin to embrace the truth that the hands that hold the handlebars and the hands that hold the seat are the same hands.

This is the sum total of what you came into this life to learn.

Love,
God

APRIL 25

To: You

Desire is the human expression of your soul's divine plan for evolution.

When you desire something, your mind searches for ways to obtain it. There are two ways of getting something: you can purchase it, or it can be given to you.

To purchase what you desire, you must fine-tune the quality and quantity of service you render to others. This will lead to increased income for you, which you may then use to buy what you want.

To receive what you desire as a gift, you must perfect yourself such that you would qualify for what you seek. That is, you must become the sort of person who would possess what you crave. You then become an energetic match for what you desire, and it is drawn to you.

Either way, you and the rest of the world expand and grow. This is the role of desire.

Love,
God

To: You

A stone dropped into water causes ripples to spread in expanding concentric circles.

Think of your life as the surface of the water and your beliefs as the stones. What you believe about yourself, other people, situations, and even what you believe about me are all stones you toss into the water. As they spiral out, they impact your reality.

Make certain that the ripples you are experiencing are satisfying. Is your life pleasant and enjoyable overall? If so, your beliefs are in line with your highest self. If not, know that you have the power to change the ripples of effects by changing the stones of beliefs.

You will always have beliefs; therefore, you will always be tossing stones. What is the most loving thought you can believe? Dwell upon the answer to this question, let this become your belief, and the ripples you experience will be pure bliss.

Love,
God

APRIL 27

To: You

The power of prayer is not that it moves me to do what you ask.

The power of prayer is that it reminds you that I am here, providing all that you need.

Sometimes prayer inspires you to take action, and at other times it leads you to simply let go and let things unfold.

Prayer invites you to hear your own perspective on a situation and then to consider mine.

Prayer evokes your highest self.

Prayer blankets difficulty in pure potential.

Prayer is an affirmation that every challenge has a solution.

Prayer reminds you that there is a loving force behind all that you see.

Prayer is this and so much more.

Love,
God

APRIL 28

To: You

You walk never thinking how to move your legs.

You listen without forcing your ears to attune to sound.

You see without urging your eyes to focus.

And you live enfolded in my grace without having to do or be anything other than who you are.

Do not seek to please me, my precious child, for your very existence does that completely.

Love,
God

To: You

In time, all will heal.

In time, all will be revealed.

In time, all will awaken.

In time, peace will reign.

In time, love will flourish.

In time, the time is now.

Love,
God

APRIL 30

To: You

Witness what you call nature.

In the midst of the blazing summer sun, does the tree doubt that very soon there will be a cooling autumn?

During the depths of a frozen winter, does the stream fret over whether there will come a thaw?

You have the power of doubt. Your doubt robs you of the present by focusing your gaze on an undesirable and, as yet, unformed future.

You also have the power of faith. Faith brings you peace and opens your heart to receive your forthcoming good.

This day, be aware of your doubts, and overlay them with faith.

Love,
God

MAY

Do

Thoughts without action are empty.
Love without action is wasted.
Desire without action is unfulfilled.
Intention without action is moot.
Prayer without action is anemic.

Action is both the spark that ignites the fire
and the hand that strikes the spark.

Action is the fulfillment of knowledge, the
realization of desire, and the demonstration
of life.

To: You

Every hero is victorious over seemingly insurmountable odds.

A hero perseveres in the face of doubt, opposition, and uphill battles.
A hero doesn't give up—no matter what.

Rarely do heroes fully grasp their capacity until they are tested. It is the
very test that reveals the hero's strength and power.

In a sense, the struggle itself creates the hero.

This day, give thanks for your struggles and difficulties. They shake your
soul and release your glory.

Have faith. Keep going. Know that I am with you just as I've been with
every truly remarkable hero.

Love,
God

Do
MAY 2

To: You

"Can't."

This word echoes in every corner of your world, and it amazes me when I hear it. Especially when people say they can't do something they have never attempted.

If people have never tried something, how do they know they can't do it?

"Can't" is often used as a subtle way of saying "won't" while simultaneously attempting to save face.

When a bird is but a nestling, it has yet to fly.
This doesn't mean it can't fly.
Just because you have yet to successfully do something, even if you've
   tried repeatedly, doesn't mean you can't.

This day, trade in "can't" for "have yet to." You are still growing and changing. What seems impossible is moving within your reach.

Love,
God

To: You

You stand before a large, impressive door.

You long for what is on the other side.
You imagine it as yours.

You can hear others inside, enjoying the bounty that awaits you.
You feel nervous excitement for what is surely to come.

And yet you just stand in front of the door.

You ask me to bring you what's behind the door.
You complain to others about the unfairness of not receiving your heart's
 desire.
You stare anxiously at the clock as time slips by.
You breathe a resigned and exasperated sigh.

You withdraw and walk away, leaving everything untouched, unexplored,
and unenjoyed, when all you ever had to do was walk through the door.

Open the door today. Walk through it to your heart's desire.

Love,
God

Do
MAY 4

To: You

Fingers darting like a hummingbird, a violinist summons forth a spirited melody, shivering twenty thousand spines in the audience.

Twisting, arching, seemingly unbound by gravity, an athlete gracefully slips the basketball past a wall of giants for a slam dunk.

Squalid, filth-laden prison walls house a small woman—gentle as a dove—for decades, until she leads her nation in triumphant revolution.

You view such people and wonder if I somehow favor them. You feel they must be imbued with special abilities and gifts.

They are not.

What sets these individuals apart is that they have prepared themselves for their moment.

Then, when the moment came, they had the courage to accept it.

Your moment is coming.
Begin today to prepare.

Love,
God

To: You

To appreciate the meal,
savor every bite.

To magnify the romance,
give yourself completely to each kiss.

To abide in beauty,
drink in its presence.

To enjoy dear friends,
open your heart.

To experience sacredness,
remember that you carry it within you.

To fully enjoy the destination,
seek joy in your steps toward it.

To have lived a happy life,
experience happiness in each day.

Love,
God

To: You

Imagine your soul as a garment.

Throughout life's journey you have picked up things and placed them into your soul's pockets.

You have picked up experiences—experiences you can share for the benefit of others.

You have picked up debts—debts in the form of help you have received, which can only be repaid by helping others.

You have picked up knowledge—knowledge that has no value until it is put to work improving your family, your neighborhood, your world.

At some point, you will lay down this body that has been home for your spirit.

Die with your soul's pockets empty.
True wealth is measured by what one gives away.

Love,
God

To: You

You long for a day when there are no problems—no issues to face, no difficulties to resolve, no challenges to overcome, no setbacks to endure.

You yearn for a time when you, your family, your friends, and your world are free from complications, strife, and tribulations.

Know this: that day will not come.

Why?

Because it is in facing your issues that you grow and expand.
In resolving difficulties, you experience a sense of accomplishment and meaning.
In overcoming challenges, you discover just how powerful you are.
In enduring setbacks, you take your greatest steps forward.

Do your best to make things better, but know that future generations will have their work to do, and this is by design.

There is a perfect plan inherent in life's imperfections. In your efforts to make your world whole, you will discover your wholeness.

Love,
God

MAY 8

To: You

That which is most crucial you will find very difficult to do at the time it is most needed.

To apologize during the white heat of an argument.
To forgive when your heart has been trampled.
To listen when your mouth burns to speak.
To remain calm while others rant.
To trust your guidance in the face of strong opposition.
To believe when all hope seems lost.
To breathe deeply when anxiety threatens to overwhelm.
To slow down when you are busy.
To let an offense pass at the moment it occurs.
To embrace when you want to push away.
To give when you feel you do not have enough.

Each action taken when it seems most difficult taps into a deeper reservoir of strength and calls forth infinite, divine nature—the truth of who you are.

What are you resisting now?
It is a call for you to act.

Love,
God

To: You

A colony of bees.

There are scouts, nurses, workers, and a queen. There are bees that build the hive and others that protect it. There are individual bees that collect the pollen and those that make the honey. Each has its role, and each performs its task.

The workers do not envy the scouts; the honey makers don't long to be a queen; the scouts don't want to change jobs and construct the hive.

In the absence of comparison with others, each bee is content.

You have skills and talents uniquely your own.
You have a passion for something, although you may not yet have discovered it.
You engage in activities that bring you joy—activities that can become your vocation.

There is a role you were born to play.

Unlike the bees, you get to discern your calling.
Just like the bees, you will be happy to the extent that you do not envy another person's position.

Love,
God

MAY 10

To: You

A young bird stands at the edge of its nest. Below is what appears to be infinite space; at the bottom is hard ground. Although the fledgling was born to fly, flight seems impossible.

An infant pulls herself up to a standing position. She extends one wobbly leg and shifts her weight but does not step. Walking seems impossible.

A man stands backstage, preparing to speak to a large gathering. His hands are sweating, his mouth is dry, his mind is a blaring cacophonous din of fearful thoughts. Addressing the huge audience seems impossible.

A moment later the bird flies, the infant walks, and the man speaks.

Everything is impossible until it is done. It is the act that calls forth the capacity.

If you are waiting for something to become possible before taking action, know that it is action that makes things possible.

Love,
God

MAY 11

To: You

What do I do first? Page 2.

What should I avoid? Page 4.

What do I do if things aren't working? Page 36.

Thus reads the table of contents of a typical owner's manual.

Life doesn't come with an owner's manual.

You do not live to follow a manual. You live to write an autobiography—a history of your successes and failures, struggles and celebrations, inspirations and lessons.

You are not here to follow instructions; you are here to discover, experience, and enjoy.

You are not here to follow a path; you are here to blaze a trail.

You are here to write an epic.

Love,
God

MAY 12

To: You

You stand looking up at a large mountain—its peak seeming to scrape the sky, its summit well beyond your reach.

Taking a breath, you place one foot on the mountain path and take a step up—just one step.

Then you take another and another. In time, you look down and marvel at how far you have climbed. Yet when you look up, the pinnacle still seems so distant.

You now have a choice: climb down or continue. You decide to keep going.

In far less time than you imagined, you are seated atop the peak, drinking in the sweeping landscape from horizon to horizon. Taking just one step at a time, you have made it.

Are you gazing up at a daunting climb?
Are you somewhere mid-journey?
Are you nearing the top?

Wherever you are, simply take the next step and know that I will be there to guide you, love you, support you, and celebrate your every stride.

Love,
God

MAY 13

To: You

Opportunities rarely present themselves as inviting alternatives.

Rather, they tend to show up as challenges, inconveniences, distractions, and even irritations.

An opportunity may even back you into a corner, giving you no other choice but to explore its rewards.

This is because your soul does not want to miss the opportunity.

Consider the opportunities available to you, packaged as they may be as distractions or inconveniences. If one appears as a nice idea you might consider, then you may or may not take advantage of it. However, if it shows up as an urgent problem, you have to address it and, in so doing, harvest the blessing contained therein.

Challenges awaken you to a better way. They are indications of opportunities beckoning you. This day, give thanks for what you call problems, and know them for what they are—the seeds of opportunities.

Love,
God

To: You

What would you do if you were in a boat that was beginning to take on water?

You'd bail the water out to prevent the boat from sinking, right?

But would you wait until the water level in the boat was dangerously high, or would you begin to bail at the first sign of a leak?

Ideally, you would begin to remove the water as soon as you notice it.

This is how you maintain your center of peace, calm, and happiness. When you begin to feel tense, upset, or unhappy, don't wait until you are up to your neck. Breathe deeply, pray, journal, walk away, do whatever it takes to keep your emotional state fully afloat.

It's much easier to bail out a little water. It's much easier to raise your spirits before they sink too low.

Today, watch for any signs that you are starting to founder. As soon as you notice a leak in your emotional hull, start bailing.

Love,
God

To: You

Right now, wind is blowing in many areas around the world. But is the wind all blowing in the same direction?

Of course not.

There is an overall pattern of wind energy, but at any given moment, somewhere on the earth, wind is moving east, west, south, north, and every direction in between.

Consider the sailor who refuses to raise his sail until all the earth's winds are unified in the direction of his voyage. He would wait forever and never leave port.

If you wait until all conditions are favorable for your endeavor, you will never begin. You don't need all winds moving you forward, only enough wind to carry you to your next port.

Begin now. Cease to wait. Taking action makes conditions favorable.

Love,
God

To: You

Do not cry out.
Speak up.

Crying out is lamenting how terrible things are.
Speaking up is pointing out how things might be improved.

Crying out is placing blame on someone else.
Speaking up is taking responsibility for making things better.

Crying out shouts in every direction at everyone.
Speaking up is directed toward those who can make things better.

Crying out says, "This is bad! Someone should fix it."
Speaking up says, "This can be improved. How can I help?"

This day, do not cry out. Speak up.

Love,
God

MAY 17

To: You

The higher you climb a tall ladder, the farther you can see.

You have within your soul a ladder. You may have found a comfortable resting spot upon this ladder, but know that there are much loftier perches awaiting you. From these higher elevations you can see much farther—new possibilities and brighter vistas.

How do you move higher up this internal ladder? First, embrace the truth that there are levels of spiritual awareness you have not yet explored.

Second, make a commitment now to climb to the next rung—just to the next rung. Don't attempt to climb too high too quickly. Adjust to the new altitude, and then climb to the next rung.

You alone select the level of emotional and spiritual heights you experience.

Make a decision; take a step up.
Enjoy the view.
Rest.
Take another step.

Love,
God

MAY 18

To: You

If you stand in a dark room while looking through a kaleidoscope, you will see nothing.

However, when you step out into the light, the view within the kaleidoscope explodes into shimmering radiant shards of ever-changing color.

What was once dark and uninteresting becomes a brilliant display.

Your life is a kaleidoscope. When you focus your life toward my light, it looks dazzling and exquisite.

This day, look beyond darkness and fear.

Let there be light!

Love,
God

To: You

Sometimes the most important thing you can do is nothing.

When you can't be your most loving self, no action you take or statement you make will improve a situation.

In those moments, do nothing. Wait until you feel replenished and capable of addressing the issue with peace and confidence.

When you sit quietly in the midst of turmoil, you are not being weak; you are showing the greatest of strengths—restraint.

This day, consciously do nothing when to do something would not be productive. Develop a sense for these times and release yourself from conflict both internally and externally.

Love,
God

MAY 20

To: You

Lightning explodes across a black sky, searing a momentary image into your mind. It is here and gone almost before you register its presence.

Thunder rumbles along to catch up—the concussion from this celestial firework shaking your windows and thumping your chest.

It is no coincidence profound insight is also called a flash. Like lightning, it comes powerfully into your darkened consciousness but departs quickly, leaving only a dim aftereffect.

If you will recognize your flashes of insight and begin to act on them, your action, like the thunder, will shake the ground and build as it rolls along.

The lightning crack is the easy part. Harnessing the thunder by taking action is the only way to turn this powerful flash into enduring substance.

This day, as you receive a flash of insight, act!

Love,
God

To: You

If no one were judging you, what would you do?

If no one was approving or disapproving of you, how would you live?

If no one praised or criticized you, how would you fill your days?

When you can answer these questions and live within these parameters, you will be free.

And, ironically, it is when you no longer care whether others approve of you that you will receive their adoration and admiration. However, you will be so focused on living for the joy of living, you will not even notice.

This day, free yourself by spending some time asking and answering the questions above.

Love,
God

MAY 22

To: You

Speak and you will find your voice.

It is not until you open your mouth and allow your words to spill forth like seeds from a granary that you will discover all that you have to say and how eloquently you can say it.

Your words can move others, comfort them, inspire them, and guide them. They are valuable coins waiting to be offered up for the betterment of all.

Don't wait until you are ready, for you never will be. When you feel guided to speak—speak! And know that I will guide not only what you say but also how it is heard.

Love,
God

To: You

Come with me.

I am walking just ahead of you—always in sight and never more than a pace or two ahead.

Be calm—you cannot stray from my path, for I am everywhere. And when you consciously walk with me, you travel in bliss.

Here I am. Take my hand. Take the next step, and together we will have an inspiring walk.

Walk with me this day, for I have amazing things to show you.

Love,
God

To: You

As long as you continue to attempt, you learn, you grow, and you move toward what you seek.

Failure is a word often used when a more accurate term would be *giving up*. Never give up on what is important to you.

For example, do you desire a healthy body? Hold an image in your mind of the body you desire and live as a person who already has such a physique. Continue this practice until your ideal and reality merge.

How long might this take? As long as is necessary.

You will reach your dream so long as you stay with it. Only you can remove yourself from progressing toward your aim.

Expand yourself.
Do something, however small, this day to move toward your ideal, and
    celebrate your progress along the way.
You are closer than you think.

Love,
God

To: You

Savor this day.

If you knew you would not receive any more days to enjoy, then this day would be a delicious experience. For all you know, this may be your last day in this mortal form, so embrace everything that is and everyone you know.

In the final moments before you close your eyes forever, you will not regret the tasks you have left incomplete.
You will not feel sad for the meetings you did not attend.
You will not lament missing the television shows you DVR'd.

But you may feel a tinge of regret for the damaged relationships you have not healed.
You may feel sad for not having another day with your children.
You may lament missing another sunrise.

Before this day begins, write on a piece of paper, "If this were my final day, I would…" and then live as if today were your last.

I promise you a magical and transformative twenty-four hours.

Love,
God

To: You

It is impossible for you to do something you know to be wrong.

You may doubt this, but it is true. Prior to doing something you consider wrong, you will rationalize as to why it is the proper course of action. Then, feeling justified, you proceed.

You rationalize to convince yourself that what is wrong is actually right by telling yourself rational lies.

Rather than depleting your energy in such a way, ask your heart what is right and have the courage to follow your guidance.

Taking the path you are guided to follow is always the easiest trek because there are fewer obstacles along the way and you feel energized by your own authenticity.

This day, notice when you tell yourself rational lies. Then close your eyes, listen to your heart, and follow your guidance.

Love,
God

To: You

Far ahead there is a distant horizon shining before you.

This bright vista beckons you to approach, but as you do, it seems to withdraw. You plead, "Am I to walk this path forever seeing ahead that which calls me forward and yet never reaching it?"

Oh, my dear child, this glimmering vision seems always ahead, but if you would look around you now, you will see that you have made great progress toward it. Countless steps along your journey have passed silently beneath your feet and you missed them because your focus remains out in the misty distance.

Right now, the shining future you prayed for has arrived. Can you pull your ship into the harbor of this moment, breathe, and enjoy? If you can, you will take pleasure in all that life brings.

This day, realize that the future to which you aspire is here now and that the only joy you will ever know is also present and within your grasp.

Love,
God

Do

MAY 28

To: You

Call forth what you need.

If you need power, do not wrestle it from another; call it forth from within yourself. It is there.

Do not seek money from the world; call forth your ability to share your talents and skills, and money will flow to you.

If you want love, do not court it from others. Share love from your heart, and the world will respond.

Everything you need sleeps within the depths of your soul, awaiting your call. This day, call forth what you desire.

Love,
God

MAY 29

To: You

Keep on. You'll make it.

The dream that shimmers before you awaits your arrival.

Oh, you may play the game along the way of creating roadblocks to test your resolve or to make your ultimate success feel that much more thrilling. But you will reach your ideal so long as you continue moving forward.

Your dreams are my gift to you.
They beckon you forward into new experiences.
In those new experiences you glimpse ever more fully our oneness.

Take the next step. Today, press on.

Love,
God

Do
MAY 30

To: You

There is perceived safety in following.

You think that others who go before you must have insights and answers, and so you follow them.

Every moment of every day is unique. To follow another is to walk along a forgotten and overgrown path.

Follow no other person.
Follow your own heart.

Love,
God

To: You

If you could pause all activity in the world and do whatever you wish, what would you choose?

If the spinning cycle that is your life were stopped for twenty-four hours, what would you do to fill your time?

The answer to these questions invites you to discover new meaning and peace.

Sometimes you choose illness as a way of pausing your life and allowing yourself to simply be. And yet you needn't put your body through the stress and struggle of sickness to achieve this rejuvenated perspective.

This moment, ask yourself, if everything were to stop for twenty-four hours, what would I do? Then courageously do those very things, for they are your soul's longing to express the truth of who you are.

Love,
God

Transform

Everything is transforming, shifting from one way of being to another.

As transformation occurs, you call forth your latent capacity to create wonders, handle challenges, and adapt to new experiences.

Just as you have gone through many versions of your physical form and yet have remained unchanged, there will be many varied expressions of your mental, emotional, and spiritual form, but you remain unchanged at your core.

At your center, you are love, and love's reward is peace.

Peace, therefore, is the ultimate destination of life's unending game of transformation.

JUNE 1

To: You

You struggle today.

You worry about tomorrow.

And yet you look back and reminisce fondly about yesterday.

If you could see the absurdity of this pattern, you could shift your perspective and begin to fully enjoy life.

The challenges you face today will one day become a source of pride for having been successfully overcome.

The tomorrow you fear will bring to you new people, new opportunities, new learning, new growth, and new experiences of every type.

Knowing this will turn your yesterdays into precious gems strung into a dazzling necklace that is your life.

Love,
God

To: You

The seed that nestles in the soil is transforming into a sprout.

The baby that sleeps in the crib will soon walk out into the world.

Whatever is, is changing.

Strive though you may to prevent change, change always wins.

When you embrace the transitory nature of all things, you begin to appreciate what you now have because everything is only for now.

Whatever is bringing you joy will change.
Whatever is causing you consternation will change.

Accept this reality, sit back, and begin to enjoy the ride.

Love,
God

To: You

Your fingers caress a silken strand spun from pure gold.

You reflect on how much you are loved, and as you do, without realizing it, you begin winding a small ball of golden thread.

You help someone in need and, at the same time, wrap another strand around the ball.

You forgive someone for disappointing you and make another pass with the thread. The ball begins to grow.

You sit and contemplate your blessings and wind another loop around the ball, which continues to expand.

You take a deep breath rather than reacting in anger and again add another golden layer to the ball.

Soon you look down and realize that you now hold a gold ball of enormous wealth created by small, seemingly insignificant threads of kindness, helpfulness, forgiveness, generosity, understanding, compassion, and gratitude.

A life of value is created one golden strand at a time.

Love,
God

To: You

Rainwater trickles down a city street and disappears into a gutter, where it is routed and diverted through a series of underground pipes. Churning and bubbling, the water eventually spills out into a large reservoir.

Here the water rests in stillness for a time. Then the warmth of the sun changes it into vapor.

Higher and higher the water vapor rises, ultimately forming clouds. As the clouds become heavy with water, they open up and spill down to the ground, nourishing plants and animals.

Then the whole process begins again.

There is a cycle to water. There is a cycle to life. Both cycles are examples of unceasing change.

If you are twisting and turning in darkness, you will, in time, emerge into the light.
If you are resting peacefully, in time life will raise you up.
If you are soaring high, you will cascade down for a period of time.
Then you will repeat the process.

Wherever you are, know that it will change.
Wherever you are, give thanks.

Love,
God

To: You

"Why is this happening?" is a question that cannot be answered. It is a recipe missing its most crucial ingredient: time.

Time is a filter through which experiences pass, contextualizing them and providing increased understanding.

Gazing through the lens of time, you discover that
    struggles ignited your innate power,
    detractors became benefactors,
    failures became lessons,
    enemies became allies,
    pain became fertile ground for growth.

Seek the blessings in your past experiences, and you will find that they always arrive in a gift-wrapped box labeled Time.

Love,
God

JUNE 6

To: You

Copper ore slumbers in the ground for millennia before being mined to the surface, where it is smelted and combined with tin to make bronze. The bronze is then molded and shaped into a magnificent statue that simultaneously touches the heavens and conveys their glory.

Years pass, then decades and centuries. The once awe-inspiring statue becomes commonplace to the point of going unnoticed.

A war breaks out, and the statue is demolished. The bronze is melted and transformed—this time into swords.

In the hands of an artist, the bronze inspires and enlightens; in the hands of a sword maker, it becomes an instrument of death. However, the basic nature of the ore never changed.

You, my divine one, are such as the ore—filled with limitless possibilities. Through the heat of life's challenges, you are melted into pliability. Then, through your thoughts, words, and actions, you choose your new form.

What are you choosing to be this day?

Love,
God

To: You

If I could put my arms around you, I would.
But that would mean that I am outside of you rather than one with
every cell of your being.

If I could speak to you, I would.
But that would set my voice apart from the sounds of nature and the
voices of others.

If I could hold your hand during times of trouble, I would.
But that would close your grasp just when your hands need to be open
and reaching.

If I could guarantee you a pain-free tomorrow, I would.
But that would only serve to rob you of the growth and clarity difficult
experiences bring.

If I could convince you that you are loved, guided, and lack nothing just
as you are, I would.
For, indeed, that is the truth.

Love,
God

JUNE 8

To: You

You wait in line at the bank. As a teller motions you forward, you smile and present a check to be cashed.

Examining the check, the teller notes that it is properly filled out and endorsed. Nonetheless, he refuses to cash it for you.

"Why not?" you ask.
"Because this check has already been cashed," he replies.

A check is valuable only until you withdraw its value. The same is true for a day in your life.

Right now, you hold in your hand a check made out to you, dated today, and signed by me. And, thus far, the amount line has yet to be filled out. Decide now on the value you will receive from this day.

Leave behind both the gains and losses of the past, for they are cashed checks.

Set your intention on high yields today; have the courage to claim what you will have, and it will be yours.

Love,
God

To: You

What if life were like Facebook?

What if you could click Like and some person or thing would become more prominent in your life? Or simply click Unlike and remove something or someone?

Actually, life is exactly like Facebook. You Like people and experiences with your focused attention, and they become part of your daily news feed—that is, your life. If you wish something or someone gone, simply Unlike it or them by withdrawing your attention.

You may wonder, *If this is true, why do so many people suffer through difficult relationships and situations?*

It is because people have added a third option: Dislike. Clicking Dislike increases one's irritation at certain people and situations while simultaneously increasing the frequency with which such people and things show up.

This day, like and unlike what you will, but refrain from disliking anyone or anything.

Love,
God

Transform
JUNE 10

To: You

This day, you begin a new chapter in your life.

I have arranged for an experience to occur that will springboard you
in an exciting new direction. When it happens, it may at first appear
to be challenging or even frustrating, but remember that it is a launching pad for your greater fulfillment.

Be open to what transpires this day.

It will mean a shift in your awareness which will draw you even closer
to your highest aspirations—your grandest expression.

You are ready.

Now is the time.

Love,
God

JUNE 11

To: You

Your mind is like a puppy.

It has the potential to be trained and to do as you instruct, but most people do not make the effort to discipline their minds.

Just as training a puppy takes time, patience, and repeated effort, the same is true for the mind. To give over to habit and let the mind jump on the furniture, tear things up, and soil your environment only leads to aggravation and frustration, which perpetuates its poor behavior.

The undisciplined mind grows into a big, old dog that resists your attempts at training. With repeated effort, however, your old dog can learn.

Take your mind for a walk with fantasies and dreams.
Let your mind play with jokes and lighthearted ideas.
But also mix in discipline so that you become master of your mind.

Develop focus little by little. Soon, when your mind gets unruly, you will be able to simply command it to stay.

Love,
God

To: You

Skilled hands apply the last delicate coat of clear glaze to a figurine.

Untold hours have gone into mixing the slip, pouring the mold, and sanding its edges smooth. The master's brushes—some only a few hairs wide—apply glaze, adding color, depth, and shading.

The work is complete, and yet the transformation is not. There must come one more thing—fire. Intense, scorching, raging fire will melt the glaze to a dazzling glass-like appearance.

It is no accident that so many great spiritual teachers selected fire to symbolize transformation.

The master may create a beautiful work of art, but the fire transforms it into something spectacular.

If you are feeling scorched by life, know that it is the refining fire of transformation, and have faith that through this process you will be reborn stronger and more beautiful.

Love,
God

Transform
JUNE 13

To: You

Adopting new beliefs leads to new actions.
New actions change outcomes.

If you believe that you are capable, important, and powerful, your actions
will reflect these beliefs. You will behave competently and boldly because
you believe this is your nature.

If, however, you believe that you are inferior, limited, and incapable,
your actions will reflect this belief and such will be your reality.

My divine expression, you have chosen what you believe about yourself.
To transform your life, you must first transform your thoughts about the
person whose life it is. Encourage an unending stream of positive words
and statements about yourself to run through your mind.

As you chant praise and appreciation for yourself, notice how easy
it is to take action that supports your grandest aspirations.

Love,
God

JUNE 14

To: You

Consider your hand.

It is not the same hand of decades gone by.

When you were a child, your hand was small, delicate, and uncoordinated. It was too tiny to grasp something large, too weak to lift anything substantial, and too unsteady to manipulate something small.

Now your hand is bigger—it is strong, skilled, and confident. With it, you reach high above your head to get what you want. With this hand, you hold on to what you value.

Within the unsteadiness of your youthful hand was the full potential for all that your hand is now. It simply needed time to grow and develop.

Within your mind and your heart is the capacity to do, embrace, and endure all things, and even now you are growing into that capacity.

I have blessed your hands, your mind, and your heart to be everything you will need.

Love,
God

To: You

Consider playing a computer game. You get to a new level and discover that it is more challenging than any previous one. However, the very fact that it is more difficult keeps you engaged.

You become preoccupied with mastering this new, more challenging level. You find yourself reaching for the game frequently, your desire to be victorious consuming you.

Finally, through trial and error you prevail. You conquer the challenges; you master the skills of your current level.

How are you rewarded? You go on to an even more challenging level.

It is this progression that keeps you actively involved in the game. If you were to go back to previous levels, you could move quickly through them, but you would also become bored and not have fun.

When each day seems more challenging than the day before, give thanks. Life is your soul's version of a computer game. And just as most video games have cheat codes to help the player move more quickly through a level, you too have access to such a help.

It's called prayer.

Love,
God

To: You

When a butterfly is mature, it struggles from its chrysalis, dries its wings in the sun, and flies away never to return.

The delicate silken chrysalis was home for the butterfly's metamorphosis, but once the transformation is complete, it is left behind forever. In time, the empty cocoon is dissolved by wind and rain.

The painful and difficult times you have gone through are like the butterfly's empty chrysalis. There is no need to revisit those experiences. They are hollow and empty vestiges of the past—a past you no longer inhabit. Let the winds of time and the rain of forgiveness dissolve them.

This day, cease to struggle, dry your wings, and soar as the radiant butterfly you are.

Love,
God

To: You

As you look at pictures from decades past, you are surprised by how different you appear now. But as these changes were occurring, you barely took notice.

Today, you will change. In subtle, even imperceptible ways you will change from who you were just yesterday. Change is ongoing and inevitable, but know that you can direct the course of change by choosing what you wish to become.

Nothing is more powerful as a means of channeling the limitless options of change than your intention for yourself.

This day, know that you are changing—this is not optional. Therefore, harness change with your intentions. Without a clear direction, your future will be created haphazardly, and the result may not be to your liking.

Remember: change may be a certainty, but your direction of change is a choice.

Love,
God

Transform
JUNE 18

To: You

I have given you the power to name everything.

With your voice you declare to yourself and others what a thing, person, or situation is.

Whereas someone might dwell on what they call a crisis, you may choose to call the same experience a challenge, making it a stimulating occurrence rather than an overwhelming one.

Someone who annoys you may be designated either a troubled person or a pain in the neck. Either tag will dictate how you treat this person and, ultimately, how they treat you.

Is the loss of something a tragedy or an opportunity?

Is unanticipated good fortune a fluke or proof of God's blessings?

This day, choose your words with great care, for you will live out their underlying meaning and intent.

Love,
God

JUNE 19

To: You

A spiritual master has learned to master his own spirit.

Whenever fear and anger arise, the master quells them with a confident "Peace, be still." In that moment, his breathing becomes deeper, his heart rate slows, and his mind ceases to thrash about. The master is at peace, serene in the knowledge that all is, ultimately, well.

To reach such a lofty state, you must repeatedly choose to rise above pettiness and fear and to view life and others with the eyes of faith and compassion. As you open up to the unity and perfection in everything, your spirit is corralled, harnessed, and tamed. You become the master.

What would a spiritual master do in this situation? Let this question roll back and forth through your mind, especially during difficult times. As you begin to master your spirit, you will move toward spiritual mastery.

Love,
God

To: You

If you are cut, your body will instantly begin to form a protective layer over the wound and to heal.

When something painful happens in your life, such as a major disappointment or the loss of someone or something you value, in that very moment, your spirit begins to heal. And just like the cut on your physical body, it will take time.

Do what you can during your recovery not to reopen the wound by exposing yourself to what hurt you. Allow yourself the time and environment to heal.

Remember this day that the word *heal* means to "return to wholeness." Your body and your spirit know the path to wholeness well and will, time and again, carry you there safely.

Love,
God

To: You

A decision to see your life as a glass half full as opposed to a glass half empty will shift your perspective, bringing you greater joy.

The truth, however, is far grander than this.

If you were to sit and write down everything going well in your life—everything—and then sit and write out everything not going as you would like, you would discover that your life is actually a glass 97 percent full.

Ah, but what about the remaining 3 percent?

It is here that you are growing. This is the space in which your life is shifting. This 3 percent is where you are expanding your capacity for things to become even better, and with this increased capacity, you invoke and embrace more and more goodness.

This day, realize that seeing your life as a glass half full is a good start but falls far short of the actual truth. You are immersed in goodness!

Love,
God

To: You

Today is fresh.

Today may seem to be a continuation of all that came before, but that is only your desire to string together events in an attempt to create context.

Separate the past from the present, for indeed, any connection between them is only in your mind.

This day is untouched, unblemished, brimming with opportunities for fun, learning, and love.

As you begin this day, attempt to see everyone with fresh eyes. See them with the eyes of compassion and appreciation.

Your habitual way of viewing your life and other people is nothing more than that—a habit.

Choose anew this day.
Call forth whatever version of reality you most desire.
It simply awaits your call.

Love,
God

To: You

Listening is harnessing both the mind and the emotions to share the same space as the soul of the one speaking.

To hear is to register what is being said even if the mind is engaged elsewhere. To listen is to absorb the full impact of what is being spoken.

Listening requires engaging both your mind and emotions.

Your mind can be likened to the closed captioning that scrolls along the bottom of a television screen. However, unlike closed captions that repeat verbatim what is being said, your mind flashes observations, judgments, commentary, to-do lists, and more, even while you are supposedly listening to someone speak.

To master the art of listening, transform the inner commentary that scrolls along the screen of your mind into a paraphrase of what the other person is saying. This will ensure you know what was said.

Then engage your heart—do your best to feel as the speaker is feeling. This will ensure you have compassion for what is being said.

Everyone deserves to be listened to—not just heard, listened to.

Love,
God

Transform
JUNE 24

To: You

This is it.

This is life. It will not get better—just different. It will not get worse—it will simply change form. However life presents itself, you are master of your experience.

Can you celebrate where you are right now? Can you be content with what is and, in so doing, release both life and yourself to transform?

If you can do this, you will find joy in each moment rather than pushing happiness off to some distant, vaporous future. You will experience love rather than cling to a desire to someday be loved.

Accept and celebrate life as it unfolds this day. Be mindful of the blessings that you have, and in so doing, open the pathway to even more.

Love,
God

To: You

Time floats gently by, and you drift upon it with little or no awareness that it is there supporting you.

As you age, time seems to accelerate, but it is not time that has sped up; rather, it is your perception of time.

When you stare at a rapidly spinning ceiling fan, the blades blur together into what appears to be a solid, swirling mass. Blink your eyes quickly, and they seem to slow down and become individually distinguishable.

When you are young, your focus is on moment-to-moment living. You are blinking at the blades of life, and they seem to meander past one by one. As you age, you begin to view life as an ongoing narrative—a spinning fan blade swirling into one rapidly moving whole.

Rediscover the perspective of youth as you dwell in the wonder of the present. Blink your eyes a bit, and slow your perspective of time.

No sense in rushing.
You're here to enjoy.

Love,
God

To: You

You fear change.
You desire change.

This is the great paradox of living, and it is also the stimulus for your soul's evolution.

You will always desire that which is different and new. However, you will often hesitate to embrace things that are uncertain.

Accept this ongoing dichotomy.
Know peace.

Love,
God

To: You

Consider people you find challenging—those you'd like to change with the wave of a magic wand.

What if, instead of wishing that they be different, you changed instead?

What if you ceased counting their shortcomings and began to look for and celebrate their gifts?

What if you removed the blindfold of expectation and saw them with the eyes of acceptance?

What if you saw their difficult behavior as a scar from an old emotional wound rather than a character flaw?

People can sense what you think about them, and they respond accordingly. Change your thoughts and actions toward someone, and the relationship you have must change as well.

Love,
God

To: You

Your worries consume your thoughts and warp your emotions.

Do you wish to see your concerns vanish like dust blown away by a spring breeze?

Then shift your focus from your own problems and concentrate instead on the difficulties others are facing. Realize that everyone is experiencing some sort of challenge, and if you put your focus on desiring that they be relieved of their challenges, you will have no time to focus on your own concerns.

This day, give single-minded attention to the challenges faced by others. Hold a vision of them being relieved of their burdens.

You will affirm the truth for them, and you will lay down your own burden in the process.

Love,
God

Transform
JUNE 29

To: You

Through stories and myths, people have reinforced their belief in a beatific realm where all is well, there is ample love and abundance, health endures uninterrupted, and harmony reigns.

Many refer to this place as heaven, and great masters have taught that heaven is to be found on earth while one is alive, rather than in the next state of being.

Know this: if you aspire to be in heaven, you must be willing to see angels.

Look about you. Do you see everyday people who at some times benefit you and other times take from you? Or do you see angels? Do you see divine beings moving about their human lives?

Take inventory of your friends, family, and coworkers. Begin now, little by little, to see each of them as angels. Then expand your vision—begin to see the divine in everyone.

The more angels you see, the more you will find yourself in heaven.

Love,
God

Transform
JUNE 30

To: You

Have you ever been through a challenging situation only to find out later that it actually brought a great blessing to you? After the initial sting, you discover that it was there to help you shift into something even better.

The loss of a job might bring about a better, more rewarding career.

A slowdown in your business might cause you to think of creative new ways of building a more solid foundation.

An argument with a loved one might result in the excavation of buried issues so that they can be healed once and for all.

A health problem might get you to slow down, reevaluate your priorities, and begin to live with intention and passion.

Whatever challenge you are experiencing now holds within it the seeds of a tremendous blessing.

This day, consider that your problems may actually be your soul's guides. They may seem to be blowing you off course, but in reality they are calling you back to life's true journey.

Love,
God

Intend

When you know where you are headed,
    resistance steps aside.
Reality reshapes itself to reflect your aim.
When watered by purpose, dormant seeds take
    root and sprout.

Your focus, your intention, your aim is your
ongoing selection of what will next become real
for you. It is the exploration of free will, the
manifestation of limitless possibilities.

Discern what you wish to intend.
Keep it free from any detracting input from
    others.
Hold your intention ever before you.

Know that whatever you are presently experiencing, you have intended.

Begin now to intend only that which brings
you greatest joy.

To: You

The purpose of fear is to save your life, not shorten it.

If there is imminent danger that requires you to fight or to flee, fear kicks adrenaline into your bloodstream to prepare your body.

However, holding a fearful mental image causes your body to sustain an adrenaline binge called stress. In time, this overdose of your own internal chemicals simply wears out your central nervous system, and your life ends prematurely.

Take a look at any problem and ask yourself if you are being called
   to stand firm or to withdraw.
Take whatever action feels right.

If neither option seems appropriate, refuse to engage in fear.

Trust the resolution to the capable hands of time.

Love,
God

JULY 2

To: You

You'll never be rich enough, old enough, young enough, fit enough, thin enough, happy enough, loved enough, famous enough, spiritual enough, respected enough, or *anything* enough.

Ah, but you are as rich as the next time you give,
    as old as you act responsibly,
    as young as you act childlike,
    as healthy as your next food choice,
    as happy as you decide to be,
    as loved as you love,
    as spiritual as your conscious connection with all,
    as respected as you respect others.

Love,
God

JULY 3

To: You

You climb into your car, turn the key, and the engine roars to life. Snapping your safety belt, you check your mirrors, shift the car into drive, and head to the store.

Time passes.
You make good progress.

Suddenly, you look around and realize that you are not driving toward the store. You are actually headed toward your place of work.

How is this possible? How could you have an intention to go one place, go through the motions to get there, and then end up headed somewhere else?

The answer is simple—your mind will always take you where you are thinking. You were thinking about work, so that's where you drove.

It is not enough to discern and intend where you want to go. You must hold your destination in your mind.

Remember, whatever you predominantly think about is the direction you are steering your life.

Love,
God

JULY 4

To: You

The traveler cannot fully experience her destination until she arrives. Prior to that, her journey's end is just a mental goal—an apparition pulling her forward along her path.

The destination must first be held in her mind before it can be reached with her feet.

With no destination set, she would simply wander forever, making little if any progress.

So let me ask, where are you headed?

What is your next destination?

Is there an objective you wish to realize? An improvement you wish to make in your life or in your world?

Know where you are headed. Although you may not see your destination until you are nearly there, it will nonetheless beckon you forward, ever forward, toward its fulfillment.

Love,
God

JULY 5

To: You

There is a formula for creation.

The things you wish to call forth simply wait for you to apply this formula.

The formula is:

$$\frac{I \times E}{T}$$

I = Intention (what you intend)

E = Enthusiasm (both your passionate belief and action)

T = Time (however long it takes)

A strong **I** (intention) multiplied by **E** (enthusiasm) over **T** (time) will transform your mind and, thereby, your reality to bring into your life what you desire.

If you perceive anything to be lacking, check the formula. Then increase whichever is necessary for the fulfillment of your desires.

Love,
God

To: You

Once an eagle spots its target, it never shifts its gaze.

Unlike its prey, the eagle's eyes are in the front of its head. This design is intentional. Rather than glancing around, the eagle looks forward, always forward, never losing sight of its aim.

You demonstrate faith when you keep your inner eye—your mental gaze—focused forward on what you want rather than letting it dart about to fearful distractions and undesirable outcomes.

Right now, is your mental gaze on what you desire, or is it casting about in fear?

The eagle's course follows its gaze.

Your life follows your mental focus.

Love,
God

JULY 7

To: You

A tender green leaf hangs from the long branch of a massive oak tree.

Soon the wind begins to blow. The leaf is lifted. It ripples, dances, twists, and turns. It shudders with the energy of the wind—first rising up and then sinking down.

The leaf is neutral, suspended high above the ground by a thin stem. It is at the mercy of the wind.

You think that you are a leaf and that life is the wind.

Know this: you have it backward.

The energy comes from you, and life rises and falls based on your thoughts, words, and actions. If something needs changing, it is not life that must shift, for life simply responds to the energy emanating from you.

Life does not happen to you.
You happen to life.

You are the wind, and you choose your direction, intensity, and longevity.

Love,
God

JULY 8

To: You

What if this was *the day*?

What if this is the day you've been waiting for?

The day when it all comes together. The day you get along perfectly with those around you. The day you feel good about yourself. The day you feel divinely connected with your spirit every step of the way. The day you feel emotionally grounded while soaring spiritually.

If you knew this to be true, how would you approach such a day? What would be your expectations?

Well, today is that day. This is the day that will be a template for all happy and successful days yet to come. This is the day that raises the bar for every area of your life. This is the day that will become the standard by which the rest of your life will be measured.

Step forth into a day bursting with goodness.

Love,
God

To: You

A slight is directed your way.

An insult is laid at your feet.

A glare is aimed in your direction.

At this point, none of these actions belong to you. They have been placed before you as bait to catch you like a fish.

You have a choice:
> You can take the bait and respond negatively, meaning you will struggle and fight.
> Or you can choose to swim past.

If the bait is not taken, the fisherman will ultimately withdraw the hook. This day, set an intention not to let the words and actions of others bait you into being caught.

Swim on by and remain free.

Love,
God

Intend
JULY 10

To: You

What you have is what you will accept.

You are like a cup into which I can only pour so much—you limit your capacity such that anything more spills over the sides.

When you were a child, your parents, friends, and teachers sought to define how much goodness you could accept. But you alone now decide your capacity for love, happiness, health, prosperity, peace, confidence, and more.

Wherever you are, whatever you have, it is a reflection of what you can accept.

Cease to limit yourself. Question your beliefs about your capacity to accept, and then stretch your mind to believe that you are worthy of more.

When the mind is sufficiently stretched, life must then follow suit.

Love,
God

JULY 11

To: You

Your mind is a seesaw.

As you add thoughts, it tips to one side or the other. The more thoughts you add, the farther it goes in that direction.

Pile on fearful thoughts, and your mind dips toward worry.

Pile on gratitude, and your mind tips toward contentment.

At any given moment, you are adding weight to the seesaw. Intentionally add thoughts that tip your mind toward the joy of living.

Love,
God

To: You

The moment you declare something impossible, it becomes impossible—for you.

When you believe that someone is unloveable, you close the doors
to your heart.
When you declare a situation hopeless, you are the one withdrawing
hope.
When you give up, you discover that you can no longer get up.

Affirm that all things are possible.
Know that all people are loveable.
Hope in the midst of uncertainty.
Get up again and again.

All power rests in your belief.

Change your belief, and open the floodgates of possibility.

Love,
God

To: You

You confuse happiness with reactive joy.

Feeling good when things go well, smiling if you are not injured or challenged—this isn't happiness. It's reactive joy.

Reactive joy is short lived, whereas happiness is a way of being that transcends what is going on. Happiness is an affirmation of the soul's understanding that it is eternal and beyond the sullying reach of human living.

Happiness comes when you decide you are happy, at that moment, regardless of what is transpiring.

Certainly there will be problems and difficulties. But remember that you cannot be happy if you magnify their importance or severity.

To be happy, diminish the challenges in your mind. Release them, and remind yourself, "I am happy."

Affirm "I am happy," and it is so.

Love,
God

Intend
JULY 14

To: You

Your intention is to be loving toward others, but sometimes you are self-absorbed and short-tempered.

Your intention is to be happy, but sometimes you feel sad.

Your intention is to be prosperous, but sometimes what you owe may appear to be more than what you have.

Your intention is to feel a connection to me, but sometimes we seem irreconcilably separate.

Beloved, do not be so hard on yourself.

Remember that the failure to realize your intention simply causes you to define it more clearly, attract it more resolutely, and, in time, enjoy it more fully.

I am here now, always, to love and help you.

Love,
God

Intend
JULY 15

To: You

If you were to bake a pie, you would first decide what type of pie you wish to make.

With this decision in mind, you would know which ingredients to include and which ones to omit.

Nutmeg might be delicious in one type of pie but not in another. Meringue might make a tasty topping for a lemon pie but might detract from the flavor of a pie made from apples.

Your decision about the type of pie dictates the ingredients, the preparation, baking time, and more.

If you are feeling an unmet hunger, consider whether or not you have clearly decided what type of pie you desire. That is to say, precisely define what it is you want in that area of your life.

As soon as you decide, we can get cooking.

Love,
God

To: You

Expectations demand what must be.
Intentions dream what can be.

An expectation is a cry to receive something.
An intention is a commitment to become something.

Expectations deplete your energy.
Intentions infuse you with energy.

Expectations loom ahead, taunting you.
Intentions pull you forward with enthusiasm.

Expectations come from the vacuum of lack and are unsatisfying even
    if they are met.
Intentions, be they met or unmet, come from a wellspring of abundance
    and bestow happiness.

This day, separate your expectations from your intentions.

Let your expectations go.
Focus upon your intentions.

Love,
God

To: You

Before a pilot takes off, she goes through a checklist to make certain everything is in proper working order.

She would never consider entrusting her life and the lives of her passengers to an aircraft that is not finely tuned.

Each morning, you awaken and slide out of your bed to begin your day. Think of your feet touching the floor as being like "wheels up" when a plane's tires leave the tarmac. It is the moment of liftoff.

Just as a pilot makes certain the plane is ready for flight, make certain you are ready for the day. Recalibrate your internal altimeter by running through your own checklist:

What am I grateful for right now?

What am I looking forward to today?

You are now fully prepped and ready to fly.

Leave everything else behind, and today will be a great trip with far less turbulence.

Love,
God

Intend

JULY 18

To: You

If you wanted to dine out, you would choose a restaurant and perhaps call ahead for a reservation.

Long before you arrive, a flurry of activity ensures that you will enjoy a delicious meal. The restaurant is cleaned, fresh tablecloths are laid, food is delivered and prepared, servers ready themselves, and a hostess steps into place to offer a warm welcome.

In life, you are the diner—you select the restaurant. Once you decide upon what you desire, preparation begins.

I am your chef, waiter, and even your hostess. I prepare your meal, serve it to you, and even greet you with a warm smile when you arrive.

What is it that you're most hungry for?

Decide and know that your table is waiting for you.

Love,
God

JULY 19

To: You

From life-saving drugs to communications satellites, not a single modern convenience was discovered in its fully formed state.

Raw materials are transformed into wondrous creations by one thing— the human imagination. It is not only the blueprint for creation, it is its catalyst as well.

Everything necessary to create a computer, cell phone, x-ray machine, and every other modern product has been present on our earth for millions of years, awaiting the spark of human imagination.

The resources to create the life you seek surround you even now. They wait for you to mine, smelt, and form them in the forge of your imagination.

Imagine what you desire, and it will be yours.

Love,
God

JULY 20

To: You

All power emanates from the depths of your soul.

When you look to the world to provide what you want, you turn your back on the wellspring of creation that flows within you.

Look and discover the fullness of the "I am," which is all powerful. Claim the "I am" with words of affirmation:

"I am strong."

"I am blessed."

"I am loved."

"I am peaceful."

"I am healthy."

"I am prosperous."

"I am giving."

"I am happy."

"I am helpful."

"I am passionate."

"I am loving."

And so it is.

Love,
God

JULY 21

To: You

Fear is always a projection into the future.

You do not fear what has already transpired; rather, you fear what might someday happen.

Fear is a cancer that spreads, devouring life's joy.

Every time a fearful thought enters your mind, replace it with an image of what you would like to have happen instead. Consider the opposite of what you fear, and set it as your mental anchor. Feel yourself fully one with this intention, and you will shake off the distraction of fear.

External events and comments from others may tempt you to move your gaze from your ideal outcome to something more "realistic."

Remember, nothing that is yet to come is based upon reality. Therefore, there can be nothing realistic about it. It has not yet been formed. Therefore, place your mind, your heart, and your unwavering attention on your desired outcome.

Leave the rest to me.

Love,
God

Intend

To: You

You give up too soon.

You set an intention and hold it as a goal. But if it seems like nothing is happening to bring forth your vision, you cease to focus upon it, thereby placing everything on hold.

Creation is continuous. To participate you must focus upon a creative outcome.

The moment you set an intention, the forces of creation begin swirling, and the shift starts. So long as you hold to your intention, that which is being created continues to develop and move toward you.

Stay with your intention until what you seek becomes fully formed and present.

Hold the vision until it is yours.
Do so, and it will happen sooner than you think.

Love,
God

To: You

Do not dwell upon scarcity.

Instead, behold the vast abundance that surrounds you even now.

Regardless of what you are experiencing, know that the only thing limiting you is your inability to stretch your mind and to focus on that which you seek.

Use your mind for more than processing what you experience. Awaken to the mind's real purpose—envisioning and thereby calling forth what can be.

This day, hold thoughts of what you desire to be already fulfilled, and it will be so.

Love,
God

Intend

JULY 24

To: You

"I feel overwhelmed."
"I feel like this isn't going to work out."
"I feel like she doesn't love me enough."

Remember, dear one, such impulses are not feelings—they are thoughts. A more accurate way of stating each of these would be:

"I think I am overwhelmed."
"I think this isn't going to work out."
"I think she doesn't love me enough."

Cease to confuse thoughts with feelings. When you claim to feel a certain way, check in to discover if you are actually thinking rather than feeling.

Then remember that you alone control what you think. Choose to think only those thoughts that bring you the happiest feelings.

Love,
God

JULY 25

To: You

If I were to grant you one wish, what would it be?

Take a moment and think on this question. What would you have me provide for you if there were no limitations?

Have you decided?

Good. Then let's make it happen.

Take a moment, close your eyes, and release this desire to me. I'll get to work on it.

Then do your part—bring your wish to mind as often as you can, and remind yourself that you and I now have an agreement that it will be fulfilled.

This day, dream big and know that nothing is too big for us.

Love,
God

Intend
JULY 26

To: You

How do you see this day going?

Before people you encounter have a chance to define your reality, do so for yourself by answering this question: how do you see this day going? Set a positive intention for yourself about this day—see it clearly. Then, when your objective is set, seal it by saying, "Amen!"

The word *amen* is not a stamp you put on a letter of prayer before sending it off to me. *Amen* simply means "and so it is." Once you set a clear idea of how you want this day to go, affirm your intention, and declare, "Amen—and so it is."

Don't get caught up in asking for what you want—claim it.

Don't question whether things will align to provide what you seek— know that they will.

Claim the power of Spirit by affirming that what you seek is so. As you move through this day, revisit your intention often, reinforcing its reality by affirming, "And so it is."

Amen.
And so it is.

Love,
God

JULY 27

To: You

I am.

"I am" is a statement of being. It is an affirmation of a perceived state. It is not the truth; rather, it is a declaration of perception.

"I am cold" does not mean your body is cold. It is a statement that your body, which is always warm, perceives coldness.

"I am unloveable" is a statement that you perceive a lack of love. It is not the truth of who you are. As my divine expression, you are love and therefore always loveable.

This day, remember that your "I am" declarations are only your perceived state, which is not always the same as the truth. The truth is that you are loved, blessed, limitless, and abundant.

Align your "I am" statements with the truth.

Love,
God

Intend
JULY 28

To: You

The bow of a boat is V-shaped to slice through water and make way for the rest of the craft. As the boat moves forward, the hull parts the water and reduces drag on the vessel, allowing it to proceed efficiently.

Knowing where you want to go by having a clear intention allows you to proceed efficiently as well. When resistance occurs, knowing where you are headed parts the waters and moves you forward with less resistance and greater ease.

What is your current heading?
To which port of call are you sailing?
What is your estimated time of arrival?

Knowing the answers to these questions parts the seas before you, making your journey safe and smooth.

Love,
God

JULY 29

To: You

If you believe you are blessed, such will be your reality.

If you believe you are cursed, such will be your life.

If you expect an unhappy conclusion to something, it will surely be yours.

If you expect a miracle, it will come.

If your mind is closed to my intercession, I will seem to never show up.

If you are open to my presence, you will experience me fully.

The fullness of life flows like water. You control the flow of life's spigot with what you believe.

Open full the power of your belief, and let the goodness of life gush freely, soaking you in its beneficence.

Love,
God

Intend

To: You

You have within your heart secret desires that you have not yet spoken aloud for even yourself to hear.

Speak your dreams, and let your ears complete the loop of understanding that will ignite your soul and make clear your path.

When you are alone, ponder this question: *What dreams have I yet to profess?* And then say them. Say them until they feel like a part of you. Say them until they pour from your mouth like water from a spigot.

"I am [whatever you aspire to be]."

"I will [whatever you wish to do]."

"I will have [whatever you desire]."

You will not feel comfortable telling the world of your intentions until you can tell yourself.

This day, speak your dreams aloud as often as you can. Let your intentions be made clear to yourself and to the world.

Love,
God

JULY 31

To: You

What, then, is *my* intention?

My intention is that you be happy.
My intention is that you be loved.
My intention is that you live your passion.
My intention is that you be at peace.
My intention is that you have enough.
My intention is that you give to those who do not.
My intention is that you discover the joy of serving others.

My intention is that you smile more, worry less, laugh more, cry less, give more, and consume less.

My intention is that you glimpse the godlike power of your intention and point it toward a happier, healthier, and more prosperous future for yourself, your world, and all humanity.

Love,
God

Transcend

What seemed a lofty and mystical ideal is now simply who you are.

What was once your spiritual ceiling has become your spiritual floor.

Towering above your head are infinite divine levels that are yet to be explored.

There are levels of awakening—levels of consciousness—that you have yet to glimpse.

They await you now.

You will climb to the next level when the current one no longer feels comfortable.

When you reach each subsequent level, you will find me there, waiting for you.

AUGUST 1

To: You

Listen to the gentle whisper of your soul.

Your soul is blind to your fearful visions, deaf to your angry rants, numb to your pain.

Your soul floats in a vibration of pure love. It is beyond all human fears and frailties, above all human wants and worries.

Your soul realizes that you must be quiet to hear its soft voice. This is part of your soul's plan, for it knows that you need quiet as much as a parched flower needs water.

Float into stillness.

Rest in quiet.

Listen—be comforted and guided by your own sacred and eternal soul.

Love,
God

To: You

Life happens and people react.
This, they say, is normal.

To be exceptional, you must be the exception to that which is normal.
You must remember that all experiences are neutral until fueled by your
interpretations. You have the final say as to how you will react and, more
important, whether or not you will react.

It may seem normal or only human to become angry when someone
treats you rudely. However, to rationalize your response as being human
locks you in the human realm—a realm of pain and suffering. In truth,
you are beyond such pettiness—you are a divine and all-powerful spirit.

When you choose to transcend the drama and discord that is the life of
so many, you will find that there are fewer things to react to and so many
more wonderful things to enjoy.

Love,
God

AUGUST 3

To: You

If you look at your bank statement, it would tell you that you currently possess a certain amount of money.

You measure the amount of money in your account by the money that is present.

Why then do you measure your life by that which is missing?

If, like a bank statement, you were to receive a "life statement" listing all your assets and blessings, it would run on for thousands of pages.

Stop longing for and feeling slighted for what you perceive to be lacking.

The only way to enjoy life is to focus on and be grateful for what is present now, in the present.

Love,
God

AUGUST 4

To: You

Giving and receiving are the same thing.

When you give, you move something from one place to another. It is never lost to you; you have simply placed it elsewhere.

If you give love, the love remains; it just resides with the recipient.

If you give money, the money does not go away; it is merely in another's pocket.

As you give, you move what you give through myriad channels—all of which are sacred. Because of this divine exchange, what you give picks up more of itself like a giant snowball rolling down a hill. More love, more money, more of whatever you have given is packed upon your gift and will be returned to you manifold.

This day, consider what you want and make sure you give it away to others. In so doing, it moves through the great channels of Spirit to be compounded and returned to you.

The more you allow to flow through you, the more you allow to flow to you.

Love,
God

To: You

Meekness is power that knows its strength.

Forgiveness is love that embraces the truth.

Patience is acceptance of divine timing.

Giving is investing in your own prosperity.

Light is darkness that has surrendered.

Passion is joy running ahead of itself.

Understanding is the tearing down of barriers.

Prayer is faith that there is one who hears and has the power to act.

Peace is an unwillingness to be baited into conflict.

Happiness is a decision made moment by moment.

Life is having fun and growing.

Love,
God

AUGUST 6

To: You

Rise in the morning.

Rise above your fears.

Rise above your limitations.

Rise to your highest glory.

Rise to the level of your greatest teacher.

Rise and greet life as it reaches out to embrace you.

Rise beyond your body and meld back into wholeness.

Love,
God

To: You

Is it the contour of a bird's wing that permits it to fly?
Or the aerodynamic shape of its body?
Maybe it's the speed with which it flaps its wings.

All of these contribute to flight, but they are secondary to what allows the bird to soar, dip, swirl, and roam freely across the sky.

Without the resistance of the air, no bird can fly.
No resistance, no flight.

You have skills, talents, abilities, dreams, desires, supportive persons, and more that contribute to your ability to soar through life. But without resistance you would never get off the ground.

You are experiencing resistance right now—resistance in the form of your own fears and uncertainties, resistance in the form of difficult people, resistance in the form of challenging situations and events.

Celebrate these resistances. When you move forward into them, they will push you aloft.

You, like the bird, soar with resistance.

Love,
God

To: You

Out of fear, indifference, or ignorance, you do something that harms another person.

Later you realize your transgression and begin to feel guilty.

Guilt serves a purpose. It is a call to heal the situation through apology, amends, or a combination of the two.

Guilt is a call to action just as hunger is a call to eat. You would not wallow in hunger nor should you wallow in guilt. To dwell in guilt is to avoid taking responsibility for what transpired and to avoid rectifying it.

Just as enduring hunger cannot fill your stomach, enduring guilt cannot heal a painful situation.

Accept, admit, and do what you can to rectify any mistakes you have made.

Then let them go.

Once one has eaten, hunger no longer serves a purpose. Once amends have been made, guilt is useless.

Love,
God

AUGUST 9

To: You

Your hand.

Your heart.

When your hand is closed, you cannot grasp.
When your heart is closed, you cannot feel.

When your hand reaches out, it can draw what you want to you.
When your heart reaches out, it draws others to you.

When you raise your hand, you reach higher.
When you raise your heart, you reach compassion.

When you touch others with your hand, they feel your tenderness.
When you touch others with your heart, they feel the radiant love
of the universe.

When you give with your hands, you provide.
When you give with your heart, you transcend.

Love,
God

To: You

Some people think I hear their prayer requests and then decide either yes or no.

This is not correct. In reality, I never say no.

Sometimes, however, I do say, "Not now." But this is not a judgment of you, an attempt to punish you or to withhold anything from you. Rather, it is a way of making certain you are completely ready for my yes.

Young children often see adults driving cars and want to drive too. A good parent knows that to let the child take control of the car would be dangerous.

But this doesn't mean the youngster won't one day drive. It simply means the child has some growing to do before she is ready.

When my response to you is "Not now," seek to grow into the kind of person for whom my "Yes" will make sense. Become the kind of person who is ready to handle the responsibility of what you have asked for.

How can you become more this person today?

Love,
God

AUGUST 11

To: You

Wonder is not reserved for the young.

Wonder allows you to see your life with an openness and joy that can transform any experience.

When you look at other people and your life experiences with a sense of wonder, you find wonder-full things to enjoy everywhere.

This day, marvel at the beauty everywhere, embrace the perfection that abounds, listen to your heart, and hear the voice of love.

This day, choose to live a wonder-full day.

Love,
God

AUGUST 12

To: You

You can feel me with you at any time.

Simply take a moment and breathe deeply; close your eyes if you wish, and soak in my presence.

In so doing, you don't invite me in; rather, you acknowledge my eternal presence.

You and I are interwoven into a great tapestry. I cannot be separated from you, nor can you be separated from me. This day, take time to feel our connection, and as you do, notice how alive you feel.

I am here, now, forever.

Love,
God

To: You

The word "too" is a favorite limiting tool.

    "I'm too old."

    "I'm too young."

    "I'm too uneducated."

    "I'm too inflexible."

    "I'm too busy."

    "I'm too poor."

    "I'm too much like my mother."

Once one says "too," he or she expresses a degree of hopelessness that diminishes potential.

You are never "too" anything. Thinking of yourself as "too" creates an inability to change—a state of being condemned, constrained, and contained.

Beware of using the word "too" as an unconscious way of sweeping aside what you might do, have, or become.

Love,
God

AUGUST 14

To: You

Your soul knows and will always guide you if you will but listen.

Sometimes guidance invites you to step out and do something uncomfortable—this is intentional. It is how you grow.

Taking chances, exploring new options, going beyond previous limits are the things you will remember most fondly.

You will never feel nostalgic for the times you failed to try something new.

There is an adventure beckoning you now.

Your soul is your life's travel agent.
Get on board and enjoy the journey.

Love,
God

AUGUST 15

To: You

If you think I am not present in the challenge you are facing, you will not find me.

If you think your problem is outside of my realm or beyond my capacity, you will not fully experience my help.

If you feel that I judge you for the mess you are in, you shut me out.

If you believe that you are imposing on me, I can't offer support.

Know this:
I am with you always.
I can help you resolve anything.
I love you and would never judge you—you are and always will
be nothing but precious to me.

Reach out to me often. Just as you can never impose upon air by breathing it, you can never impose on me.

Love,
God

AUGUST 16

To: You

Listen.
Listen deeply.
Beyond the chatter of your mind.
Beyond the echoes of what you have heard.
Within the well of your soul, listen.
Listen and hear the eternal voice.

A voice that is calm.
A voice that is confident.
A voice that knows no fear.

Take a moment now to listen to this voice. It is there, whispering to you right now.

The voice tells you that you are loved.
It reminds you that things will work out.
It comforts you, saying there is nothing to fear.

This voice alone speaks the truth.

Listen.

Love,
God

To: You

You say,

"All that I want is to be well" when you are sick.

"All that I want is enough money" when funds are low.

"All that I want is someone to share my life with" when you are lonely.

And yet when you receive "all that I want," you find that another "all that I want" springs up to become your dominant desire.

Right now there is something you want. When you get it, there will be something else, then something else. Wants are inexhaustible.

You want a few things, but you already possess a great many things. Peace and happiness are found in minimizing "all that I want" and focusing on your "all that I have."

Love,
God

AUGUST 18

To: You

The highest aim in life is happiness.

For most, happiness is confused with extreme pleasure, but the two are not synonymous.

Pleasure is a high vibration of human energy, but it is based upon external stimuli that must ultimately fade. Even if the cause of your pleasure continues, you will adapt to it, thereby experiencing less over time.

Happiness is beyond the human condition. Happiness is not taking in what is pleasurable; happiness is taking pleasure in what is.

Happiness is an unshakable association with your true spiritual essence. Happiness is finding joy amid the difficult, the sour, the painful, the mundane, the empty, the seemingly unfair, and the fleeting.

Happiness is spiritual mastery.
It is the advanced course in living.
Happiness is the highest aim.

Happiness is, ultimately, what you are alive to experience.

Love,
God

To: You

You struggle to obtain your desires while your soul sits comfortably smiling atop a mountain of abundance.

You grit your teeth and endure someone you find challenging while your soul marvels at and loves this person.

You cling doggedly to what you know to be right while your soul glides along knowing that there are no rights and wrongs—only perspectives.

You regret what has happened while your soul gives thanks for everything because it has brought you to where you are.

You fear tomorrow while your soul dances joyously from scene to scene in this unscripted, award-winning play that is your life.

You doubt and fear while your soul rests in absolute certainty and unshakable confidence.

You think that you are what you see in the mirror, the roles that you play, and the things that you do.

In truth, my awakening child, you are, always have been, and always will be an abundant, enlightened, unshakable soul.

Love,
God

AUGUST 20

To: You

Have you ever considered that perhaps the person challenging you is actually me?

As you look at him or her, look closely, very closely.
Can you see me?

I am there as this person to shake you up, wake you up, get your attention, and inspire you to remember the truth of who you are.

The person who is bugging you right now is me.
I am calling upon you to act the part of the divine being I know you
    to be.
I am urging you to know and express peace, patience, compassion,
    forgiveness, and more, for these are fruits of the truth of who you are.

The more you live these aspects of yourself, the less I will need to rattle your cage. Just know that I love you no matter how long it takes.

Love,
God

AUGUST 21

To: You

You hear with your ears.
But you listen with your heart.

You view with your eyes.
But you see with your understanding.

You touch with your hands.
But you feel with your soul.

Your body is a portal conveying sensations.

Let your senses sample your world.
Let your spirit embrace, interpret, and celebrate what you receive.

Love,
God

AUGUST 22

To: You

Only for now.

The challenge you are facing is only for now.
The joy you are celebrating is only for now.

The tide never remains in.
It recedes to return again.

Inhale and give thanks for your blessing.

Exhale and release your burden.

Both are here only for now.

Love,
God

AUGUST 23

To: You

From beyond time and space, deep within your soul, I speak. And yet a wind whirls so loudly that you cannot hear me.

"Where is my God?" you cry. "Why can I not hear his soothing, guiding voice? Has he forgotten me?"

Beyond the gale I speak, reminding you that I am here, that you are loved and you are precious. You can never be forsaken. But my voice is drowned out by the ceaseless typhoon of your thoughts.

Pause, sit quietly and listen, and you will hear me beneath the squall.

Bid the storm cease.
Demand that there be peace.

Shhhh…
Quiet…
Ah, now you hear me.

I love you.

Love,
God

Transcend
AUGUST 24

To: You

There is a voice inside your head attuned to the frequency of drama, trauma, lack, and blame. Blind to the truth of what you truly are, it constantly seeks to distract you.

Through lies and sheer volume, it seeks to convince you that illusion is reality.

More! More! More! it cries.
I am grateful for what I have, your spirit responds.

I will get even, the voice threatens.
Peace always begins with someone; I will let it begin with me, your spirit affirms.

It's not fair! shrieks the voice.
No one is more favored than I am, your spirit remembers.

Listen for your soul's gentle voice.
Begin to hear and to remember the truth.

Love,
God

To: You

Something happens and you get upset.

You think that what happened caused your irritation, but it did not. Rather, you have a habitual way of responding, and when things occur, you react without conscious decision.

The next time something happens and you sense yourself becoming angry or upset, remember that it is not the situation that is upsetting.

Acknowledge your freedom to make a new choice:
> Choose to forgive.
> Choose to let things slide.
> Choose to think about something for which you are grateful.
> Choose to laugh.
> Choose to shrug your shoulders and smile.

What exactly you choose is unimportant; simply make a new, a different—a better—choice.

Love,
God

To: You

When you awoke, did it cross your mind to be frightened as to whether or not the sun had risen?

Of course not. The sun rises and shines its warming rays on all creation because that is what the sun does. You have no fear of the sun not making its daily appearance.

Why then do you have fear that I will not deliver you from pain, provide for you what you desire, or comfort you in times of sorrow? For these things are what I do.

This day, let the sight of your solar system's great star remind you that I, like it, can never and would never fail you. As the sun warms the body, feel the warmth of my presence in your soul.

Love,
God

AUGUST 27

To: You

There are people who will never be able to love you.

They are too wounded and are unwilling to heal. As a result, they lash out at others.

If you try to win them over, you will fail.

You cannot win their favor, but you can love them. They deserve your compassion and never your judgment.

This day, remember that those who act unlovingly toward you are wounded and hurting. Do not expect their love, but remember they need yours. In so doing, you offer the one thing that can lead them out of their darkness: love.

Love,
God

AUGUST 28

To: You

As you look back on challenges you have experienced, you realize that many of them were there to help get you back on track.

There was something you needed to change, some aspect you needed to develop, or something you needed to learn. Spirit simply got your attention with what you call a problem.

When you are in the midst of such a problem, it's difficult to embrace that it is there to instruct you. But if you will open your mind to this truth, you will lessen the severity and duration of the problems in your life.

What problem are you facing this day?
How might it be trying to get you back on track?

Be open to the guidance offered from this great teacher you call "problem." Once you gain its lesson, the teacher will go away.

Love,
God

To: You

Today you will receive guidance to move beyond something that is currently holding you back. The very advice you need to spiral higher will come to you this day, so listen closely.

Someone standing near you may make a remark that brings you a fresh insight.

A profound revelation may flash in your mind during a conversation with someone or while reading a letter or e-mail.

It may come to you via a song or even through what you call a news story.

The person sharing this insight with you has no awareness of being the messenger of your liberation. However, you will know unmistakably that what you hear was intended for you from me.

Hold in your mind that for which you seek guidance, and then listen— just listen.

Love,
God

AUGUST 30

To: You

All power must have energy behind it.

Without oxygen, a fire sputters out and becomes cold ash.
Without wind, a sail flutters still and halts a boat's progress.
Without sunlight, a plant withers and droops to the ground.

The power behind your emotional pain is the energy of your belief
that another wronged you.

Every time you tell your story of difficulty, you give oxygen to the fire
that burns your heart.

When you dwell upon slights and misdeeds, you calm the wind that
could fill your sail and move you forward.

With every thought of being a hapless victim, your resolve becomes
parched and withers on the vine.

You will experience disappointments, struggles, and even betrayals.
When you cease to give them energy, they will cease to have power
over you.

Love,
God

AUGUST 31

To: You

When light is shielded, it still shines unabated.

When you feel shrouded in darkness, your spiritual light shimmers unaffected.

Be with internal darkness but a moment, and you will know that it is a shadow cast by your mortal self. A shadow has no substance and cannot harm you.

Your light is all that is real. You shine from the depths of your soul and illuminate the world with your brilliance.

This day, let there be light.
Shine as never before.

Love,
God

September

Cultivate

Cultivate the…

> EYE of an artist
> HEART of a poet
> MIND of a scholar
> COMPASSION of a saint
> PLAYFULNESS of a clown
> WONDER of an explorer
> GRACE of royalty
> RESOURCEFULNESS of a survivor
> SERENITY of silence
> OPENNESS of a child
> PASSION of youth
> BOLDNESS of certainty
> PEACE of death
> WISDOM of age
> LOVE of a parent

…and the PERSPECTIVE OF GOD.

To: You

If you wish to save the world, first save yourself.

The most noble thing you can do is to spend time in prayer, deepening your connection with all. In so doing, you become a person for whom a healed world would be a natural fit. As you become such a person, the world about you will begin to shift.

Some strive diligently to save the planet, stop war, and end suffering as a distraction from healing the war and suffering within themselves. Their efforts, however honorable, are ineffectual because they carry the virus of discord with them into whatever change occurs.

If you wish to transform the world, make sure you invest at least as much time in your own personal transformation. As you seek to bring about heaven on earth, make certain you are an angel worthy of heaven.

This day, cultivate your own divinity. Delve into our oneness and dwell there, for in so doing, you accelerate the transformation of your planet.

Love,
God

September 2

To: You

Ever noticed how, when a child sets out to clean his room, he will often create a bigger mess first?

He will pull things out of his closet and from under his bed into the middle of his room, and there will appear to be such chaos and disorder that you wonder if any good will come of it.

A wise parent knows that this is just part of the process. If the child stays with it long enough, such activity will result not only in order but probably the relinquishing of things that no longer fit or are needed.

When your life seems chaotic and messy, know that you are simply in the middle of a process that indicates greater order is unfolding. In this process, you are identifying what no longer fits so that you can release it forever.

This day, give thanks for the mess in your life, knowing that as you stay with it, order will be established, and you will find peace.

Love,
God

To: You

A muscle grows when it is pushed beyond its limits.
A human spirit grows the same way.

A situation occurs that is more challenging, more stressful, or more painful than anything you have ever experienced. Then, just like someone who has engaged in overly strenuous physical exercise, you feel tired and sore for quite some time.

During this uncomfortable period following your challenge, you are actually growing. Your capacity for handling difficult issues is expanding. You are becoming emotionally stronger.

Painful and difficult times are catalysts for growth. They pass, leaving behind the gift of a new and greater capacity for facing even greater challenges.

You are much stronger than you can even imagine. You will grow into your capacity to deal with anything that comes your way.

And I will always be with you as your coach, friend, and cheerleader.

Love,
God

To: You

What did you learn yesterday in the school of life?

Perhaps you learned how to do something better. Or perhaps you discovered that it is best to discontinue something.

Regardless of what it is you learned, you get to take that knowledge with you today to make this day all the better.

And if you missed learning something yesterday, you'll have another chance today.

It's all a perfect system designed to help you awaken and live a more enjoyable, harmonious, and constructive life—all of which brings you greater joy and fulfillment.

Ah, there's the bell.
School's now in session!

Love,
God

SEPTEMBER 5

To: You

There is a game I see many of you play.
A game that cannot be won.

You spend your lives trying to figure out what is wrong with you—your focus is on your shortcomings, your issues, your limitations, your problems.

You say you do this in an attempt to become a better person. Sadly, you even believe that this will lead you to happiness.

Beloved one, just as you cannot dig deeper into a snowbank to find heat, you cannot dig deeper into your faults to find your value.

Are there things you can improve?
Sure.

But you are not broken, so get off the "fix me" cycle.

This day, celebrate—truly celebrate—all the wonder that is you.

Love,
God

SEPTEMBER 6

To: You

You crack open a new book and read a story about a character that is lavished with love, cherished, and supported as a child.

Moving into adolescence, she earns perfect grades, is admired by teachers and fellow students alike, and never experiences angst, heartache, or a single pimple.

As an adult, she finds true and lasting love, enjoys an idyllic and prosperous life without struggle, and dies at age one hundred, exhaling with a smile.

Would you find such a book interesting or inspiring? Stimulating? Would you root for this person? Would you enjoy such a story?

Doubtful.

Every good story has ups and downs, twists and turns, betrayal and reconciliation, separations and reunions, loss and discovery, challenges and respites.

Regardless of what transpires, have faith that your story, with all its plot shifts and character changes, is a happy one designed for your maximal enjoyment and fulfillment.

Love,
God

SEPTEMBER 7

To: You

Cultivate love.

Love is at the core of your being.
It is the essence of who you are.

You desire to feel love.
You desire to share love.

Giving love expands your spirit.
Receiving love nourishes your soul.

If love ever seems lacking, it is a call to you to share your love. When you bring love to any situation, it takes root and begins to grow.

Cultivate love.

Let love bloom and enjoy its heady fragrance.

Love,
God

SEPTEMBER 8

To: You

The ocean reaches the shore.
Mountains reach the sky.
Roots reach deep within the earth.
Sunlight reaches across the galaxy.

It is natural to reach.

When you reach, you stretch. When you stretch, you discover that you are taller than you realized.

Whatever your age, there are things that seem just beyond your reach, things that can be yours if you would but stretch toward them.

What do you aspire to be, to do, or to have?

This day, stretch just a little bit in the direction of your desires. In so doing, you will find that you are taller than you supposed, and you may be surprised to discover that what you seek is within range of your reach.

Love,
God

SEPTEMBER 9

To: You

Your life is complicated because you like it that way.

You may disagree. But let me say again that you find benefit in creating complicated situations.

Complicated situations make you feel important—they make you feel significant.

More than this, by making things complicated, you absolve yourself of the responsibility of making a definite commitment to an outcome. Keeping things complicated is a way of hedging your bets no matter what happens.

Remember that when you hedge your bets, you are subtly betting against yourself so that no matter how the game turns out, you still lose.

It's time to make some important decisions, let some things go, and simplify your life.

And relax. No matter what you decide, you and I together can fix things as we go along.

Love,
God

To: You

When you were born, you brought with you a small and gentle seed.

Deep within your soul it is waiting to blossom—the sweet fragrance of its flowers to be carried on the winds of life, calling forth smiles on the faces of many.

Your seed lies dormant within you, and if you do not plant and nourish it, it will pass silently with you when you draw your final breath.

Look within your heart; there you will find your distinctive seed. Plant it in the world, give it the warmth of your attention, and shower it with the rain of your time. It will grow and bless you and everyone you encounter.

You are the gardener as well as the seed.
Plant your seed and watch it begin to grow.

Love,
God

September 11

To: You

You want flowers.
But you do not plant flowers.
You plant seeds.

The seed becomes a sprout, which is not a flower.
The sprout becomes a stem, still not a flower.
The stem begins to bud, a potential flower, yes, but not yet one.
Lastly, a flower blossoms forth.

Every stage is part of the process to bring forth flowers.

You would not behold the sprout and curse it, "This isn't a flower!" and then cease to water it or rip it out of the ground. Sprouts, stems, buds, and every step in between are required.

Take a look at sprouts, stems, and buds that represent the growth areas of your life. Give thanks for whatever stage they are in—water and nurture them.

And get the vase ready, because beautiful flowers are coming.

Love,
God

To: You

If you can be content with what you have, you will receive more to enjoy.

If you cannot be content with what you now possess, more will only proportionately increase your discontent.

Being content is not settling for something; it's settling *into* where you are in one of the ongoing phases of your life.

Finding joy in what is, you open the door and lay out the welcome mat for still more to savor.

Take joy in all that you now possess. In so doing, open yourself up to find even greater joy and prosperity, because it most surely will come.

Love,
God

To: You

Choice.

You get to choose where you will live, whom you will be with, what career path you will follow, how you will spend your leisure time, what you will eat, and so many, many things.

However, the real power of choice comes in choosing how you will respond to the choices others make.

When people choose to do things that are not what you would want them to do, you can choose to get angry, choose to take their action as a personal slight, or choose any number of responses that leave you feeling separate and unhappy.

Or you can embrace their choices as just that—their choices.

In choosing to accept others' choices, you come to know your oneness with all and dwell in peace.

This day, choose to accept other people's choices.

Love,
God

To: You

Your life is a reflection of what you believe to be true about yourself.

If you believe you are loveable, you will be loved.
If you believe you are fortunate, good fortune will meet you at every
   turn.
If you believe you are creative, wondrous ideas will pour forth into your
   consciousness.

It works like this: You believe something about yourself, then the world
reflects your belief back to you. This then magnifies your belief. A loop
is created that feeds upon itself.

Cultivate loops that bring you joy. Begin to believe something you wish
to be true, and then seek unceasingly for evidence that supports your
new belief.

With every thought, you are either supporting an old belief loop or
creating a new one.

What you believe, you will experience.
What you experience, you will believe.

To change your experience, change your belief.

Love,
God

To: You

A leaf sprouts from a plant. Its purpose is to absorb as much light as
    possible.
The energy from the light it receives allows the plant to thrive and grow.

When the leaf has fulfilled its purpose, it will wither and fall, becoming
fertilizer for the plant. In time, other leaves will sprout to replace it.

The experiences of your life, be they what you would call good or bad,
are there for you to draw out the most light from them.

In good experiences you feel fortunate, happy, loved—that is, you
experience light. In bad times, you seek and find support, a deepening
of spirit, an appreciation for the brief tenure of such experiences—you
experience light.

Regardless of what is transpiring, remember that there is only light.

The situation, be it good or bad, will soon fall like the leaf from your
experience to fertilize your growth as new experiences come forth.

This day, resolve to know and absorb light from each and every situation.
It is there.

Love,
God

To: You

You don't glance nervously about, coveting more air than you can
breathe.
You don't look at the way other people breathe and envy their lung
capacity.
You don't fret over whether or not there will be enough air tomorrow.

You have always had enough air.
You don't fear running out.
You trust that there will always be enough.

Why then do you stress over material wealth?
Why do you envy the money other people possess?
Why do you fear running out of cash at some distant tomorrow?

Even though you have always had enough, you nonetheless worry that
someday you will experience financial lack.

Right now, take a deep breath, and notice how wealthy you are with air
to breathe.

Then realize that the same is true for financial prosperity. And just as
you must exhale to create a vacuum to draw in more air, you must give
money to create a space to call forth more.

Love,
God

SEPTEMBER 17

To: You

Call to mind someone you consider a spiritual mentor—someone who has achieved the level of spirituality you desire to reach.

Now know two things:
1. That person began right where you are and put forth the effort to develop the consciousness she achieved.
2. The same Spirit that flowed through this person also flows through you now.

Whoever it is you admire as an example of love, compassion, or enlightenment, you are united with this person in the one Spirit.

This day, feel your oneness with the great spiritual masters and commit to achieving—better yet, commit to surpassing—their example.

You honor your teachers by modeling for others that a life of wholeness is possible.

Love,
God

To: You

The universe is continuing to expand and will do so forever. Galaxies swirl outward into new and uncharted space because expansion is the nature of all living things.

Growth, expansion, moving into new areas—this is what the universe is demonstrating for you. The universe is an example for your soul so that you may know that as long as you are alive, you will grow.

The planets move into space never before occupied, and yet when they arrive, I am already there.

Fear not; as you have new experiences that call you to move in new directions, I am already there waiting on you. More than that, I am holding your hand through the experience.

This day, embrace growth and expansion as the nature of life. Cultivate an appreciation for what exists just outside your comfort zone.

Love,
God

SEPTEMBER 19

To: You

Life is not a linear progression of growing older.

Life is an ever-deepening exploration into the depths of who you are.

Forever deeper—this is the journey of the soul.

Life may seem to progress forward from youth to old age, but this is just your perspective. In actuality, life is a process through which you settle more fully into your oneness with everything.

Today, according to how you measure time, you will grow one day older.

Consider measuring this day not by its length but by its depth instead. Take note of lessons learned, challenges overcome, and limitations surpassed.

This is the true dimension of living.

Love,
God

To: You

A soul is an individualized universe. It is spun into motion and then spirals out into the void of new space.

It is the human soul's purpose to grow. Expanding your capacity in any area of life provides the growth the soul seeks. Each time you cultivate love, patience, wisdom, understanding, tolerance, forgiveness, acceptance, and generosity, your soul grows a little.

Experiences that are catalysts for your growth may sometimes seem quite challenging or even painful. Nonetheless, when they are met and overcome, you feel a sense of accomplishment. More than that, you feel even more powerful for having endured and survived.

Daily challenges are not there to test your worth. They are there to provide opportunities for your soul's purpose—growth.

Love,
God

To: You

A seed rests in a paper sleeve.

The package is blank, with no notation as to the type of seed. So the seed remains in the sleeve, unplanted, unexpressed, unfulfilled.

The seed might bring forth beautiful flowers with an intoxicating aroma.

It could produce large red tomatoes that burst with tart sweetness.

The seed could grow into a medicinal plant that could be used to treat the suffering of millions.

It could sprout fields of self-replicating grain to fill achy, swollen bellies.

The seed could do a great many things if only it were planted.

You came into this world with an unmarked sleeve of seeds. They are your gifts and talents. These seeds await your planting them in your life.

As you cultivate your seeds to full expression, you share with the world precisely what it most needs at this time. And you have a lot of fun in the process.

This day, cultivate the many seeds you have to share.

Love,
God

To: You

You have forgiven when you no longer wish to get even.

You have forgiven when you cease to desire that pain be returned with pain.

You have forgiven when you feel compassion rather than resentment.

Ah, but when you begin to see that there is nothing to forgive, then you move into mastery. For the actions of another, however hurtful, were in reality seeds for you to grow.

Be grateful for the growth that comes from deconstructing and rebuilding life.

When you fully embrace every action as a blessing, there is no more need of forgiveness.

Love,
God

SEPTEMBER 23

To: You

If you met someone who was experiencing trouble, you wouldn't be critical. You would offer your help or, at the very least, your compassion.

If someone were feeling sad or lonely and, as a result, reacted angrily, you would forgive her, knowing that she was just out of sorts.

If a friend needed time alone, you would understand and support this decision.

You are a loving, understanding, and compassionate person—with others.

Sadly, you sometimes treat the most important person in your life— yourself—as an irritation or an inconvenience. You hold yourself to standards you would never impose upon someone else.

Begin now to afford yourself the love, understanding, compassion, and support you would afford another.

This day, treat yourself as you would your most beloved friend, for indeed, that is who you are.

Love,
God

SEPTEMBER 24

To: You

Cultivate…

    happiness, and sadness will wither.

    love, and hatred will crumble.

    forgiveness, and pain will cease.

    giving, and lack will recede.

    understanding, and arguments will end.

    simplicity, and stress will melt.

Cultivate a feeling of oneness with me, and the garden that is your life will be lush, beautiful, and vibrant.

Love,
God

SEPTEMBER 25

To: You

Consider your previous triumphs over problems that seemed difficult, if not insurmountable. You have managed to keep it together during some pretty tough times.

You should be proud of yourself.
I know I'm proud of you.

Let this awareness of your resilience calm your mind and soothe your heart. Stop casting about fearfully over what may or may not occur tomorrow.

You have handled everything life has sent thus far.
You can handle whatever comes next.

Love,
God

To: You

From perceived nothingness comes an idea.
It is but a spark.

From an idea comes a belief.
It is a small, tender flame that can be easily extinguished if not fed.

From a belief, a command goes out to the universe to marshal together all manner of opportunities and resources to fulfill the idea.

Once a spark, the idea has now become a roaring, illuminating, and warming fire.

It's really that simple.

If you can open your mind to believing an idea even when nothing in your reality seems to support it at the time, the limitless supply of the ineffable universe will fulfill your request.

Notice that your word *ideal* is built upon the word *idea*. Ideas are the raw materials for an ideal life.

This day, pay attention to and adopt ideas that support your ideal life.

Love,
God

SEPTEMBER 27

To: You

It is easier to train cubs than to tame lions.

You ignore a problem as if it were a small lion cub, hoping it will wander off and no longer disturb you. Instead, it feeds and grows with each passing day into an adult lion ready to devour you.

The longer you ignore an issue, the larger it grows.

Declaw the lion that scratches incessantly at the cage of your mind. Open the door and face it now. Whatever the problem is, you and I will handle it.

Together we will turn a snarling lion into a docile house cat.

Love,
God

Cultivate

SEPTEMBER 28

To: You

Within the fruit of life rests the seeds of countless potential moments. You alone select which seeds you will cultivate.

To harvest happiness, cultivate seeds of acceptance.
To harvest joy, cultivate seeds of celebration.
To harvest love, cultivate seeds of compassion.
To harvest fulfillment, cultivate seeds of purpose.
To harvest health, cultivate seeds of wellness.
To cultivate abundance, cultivate seeds of service.

To harvest a deeper connection with me, cultivate seeds of oneness.

Love,
God

To: You

Before you begin this day, take a moment to think back to a previous day when you felt everything went well.

What was it like to feel light, capable, loved, unhurried, guided, and supported?

How did it feel to live a day that was joyous and on purpose?

Breathe in the memory of such a day and allow it to simmer in your mind.

It is no accident that you have read this message, for it is your soul's desire to experience another such pleasurable day today. Reading this is your reminder of that intention.

With the memory of an ideal day imprinted deeply in mind, enjoy all the splendor of this day!

Love,
God

September 30

To: You

Knowledge expands.

Every day you learn something. Each and every day you take in more information, and your mind seeks to organize what you learn into a usable format.

Your discoveries are fresh, but what you discover has always existed. You are opening presents that have been wrapped and sealed since the inception of time.

There are unexplored layers and depths you will reach through the windows of your current understanding.

This day, give thanks for everything you learn, and know that you are moving along a limitless path of spiritual development that stretches before you and welcomes your every step.

Love,
God

OCTOBER

flow

Wind whittles away the craggy faces of
    mountains.
Water carves deep into the rugged surface
    of the earth.

Both wind and water are unrelenting and
unstoppable.

Surging around whatever blocks their path,
both wind and water surround, embrace,
and ultimately dissolve what once stood in
their way.

Flow like wind.
Flow like water.

OCTOBER 1

To: You

Be grateful for where you are.
Have faith that even better will come.

This moment will pass. Life will flow. Both blessings and challenges will come, and I will be with you to celebrate the blessings and overcome the challenges.

Breathe.
Smile.
Relax.
Enjoy.

Happiness comes from enjoying the paradise surrounding you now.

Love,
God

Flow

OCTOBER 2

To: You

A hummingbird buzzes about from place to place. It flits here, darts there, and then zips off somewhere else.

The actions of this tiny aerial acrobat seem random and chaotic. Yet there is nothing haphazard about this brilliant little bird. It follows its instincts, doing what it must to ensure its survival.

Frenetic activity is what you most often notice in the flight of the hummingbird. Yet this vibrant creature can sit quietly for long stretches. When not feeding, it rests, at one with its surroundings.

Unlike the hummingbird, you dart about even when it is not necessary. You don't stop and savor the life you are living. Your busyness increases your adrenaline level, causing you to hurry all the more. It also brings on stress, releasing endorphins.

In short, you get a rush from rushing.

The rush of rushing masks the joy of living. Take a few moments right now to gaze about; drink in your life. Feel gratitude for what you have.

If even for just a moment—peace, be still.

Love,
God

Flow
OCTOBER 3

To: You

It is the pauses that give meaning to your words.
It is the rests that give the symphony its power.
It is the emptiness of space that frames the stars with beauty.
It is the separation that makes the homecoming joyous.

No spice makes food more delicious than the burn of an empty stomach.
No sunrise is so beautiful as the one observed breaking through
    darkness.

The stillness defines the breeze.
The lull makes the wave.
The plateau prepares one for the climb.

Cultivate quiet, stillness, and rest.

Sit.
Breathe.
Be.

Love,
God

To: You

In silence you hear your soul's gentle whisper.

As you remove outer distractions and relax past inner distractions to sit in silence, you come to know the enduring voice of your own spirit.

When you give yourself the gift of time devoid of the chatter of your world, you fill your heart with love and your mind with sunshine.

This day, take time to move apart from others and beyond the beckoning of technology to be alone in silence.

Be with me. Discover that we are truly one.

Love,
God

Flow
OCTOBER 5

To: You

Water is the most powerful force in nature. It is soft and fluid, yet carves great channels through solid rock. Water achieves its end not by force but by flowing gently.

If something blocks a stream, it does not stop. It will continue without hesitation over or around the obstacle.

If something seems to get in your way, do not waste a moment feeling upset. Whatever has blocked your path is inviting you to flow in a different direction.

Spirit, like water, is formless. And you are, at your essence, spirit. Therefore, it is your nature to flow.

This day, do not stagnate, resenting what stands in your path. Instead, flow around it and discover your true course.

Love,
God

OCTOBER 6

To: You

You breathe.
Over and over again, you breathe.

Yet you are unaware of the act of breathing.

My presence is like your breathing. In fact, for your ancestors, the word *breath* and the word *God* were the same.

Become aware of your breathing, and you automatically breathe more deeply. Your breath calms you and makes you feel more connected.

Notice my presence, and you feel more loved, more confident, and more capable.

Be aware of your breathing, and your body will relax.

Be aware of my presence, and life will relax.

Love,
God

OCTOBER 7

To: You

You inhale air that is a combination of the exhalations of millions of beings both currently alive and long departed.

You exhale, and others take in some of your breath.
Life—past, present, and future—is connected by breath.

Life is also connected by the very act of living.

Those yet to come will not only breathe your air, they will enter a world shaped by you. Your actions, your thoughts, your dreams, your words, your beliefs, your contributions—all of these will become a part of the environment for those yet to be.

Remember that you not only live but, through your life, celebrate the lives of the past and cultivate the soil from which future life will grow.

Love,
God

OCTOBER 8

To: You

A given moment might inspire joy, consternation, pleasure, confusion, and any of ten thousand other feelings.

But wrapped like a sacred gift within each moment is something for you to take hold of, to understand, to realize, or to embrace.

A moment may invite you to let the cares of today and the worries of tomorrow slip past as you revel in the presence of someone you love.

Another moment may help you discover your capacity for problem solving, compassion, or patience.

A truly profound moment may help you put into perspective the world and your place within it.

When you seek the blessing in any given moment, it spills forth.

What blessing is this moment offering you right now?

Love,
God

OCTOBER 9

To: You

Your heart pumps blood to keep you alive. Yet it does more. It maintains an internal rhythm pulsating within your body.

Thump-thump.
Thump-thump.
Thump-thump.

When you feel out of sorts, when you feel upset or afraid, take a moment and listen, really listen, to your heartbeat. Like the soft pounding of raindrops, like the soothing babble of water over rocks, your heart's unceasing rhythms will calm you, comfort you, and bring you peace.

Listen right now. Hear the gentle throb of your internal metronome, and let it echo through the rafters of your mind.

Love,
God

OCTOBER 10

To: You

The wind blows around the world.

Along its journey, it caresses the smooth, fresh faces of children as well as the wisdom-etched faces of adults.

At times the wind is balmy and warm; at others it is bitterly cold. At times it is a gentle breeze, and at others it is a roaring gale.

The wind dances, meanders, careens, rises, and falls. It scatters leaves, pushes windmills, powers ships, and sets chimes to tinkling.

Wind is strong enough to drive a turbine and gentle enough to barely flicker a candle.

You are as complex, powerful, and gentle as the wind. Your effects are felt around the world.

And like the wind, your true essence is invisible.

Love,
God

Flow

OCTOBER 11

To: You

Life appears chaotic and confusing at times, but behind the scenes there is a perfect design.

Similarly, your experiences may seem circuitous and even haphazard, but there is a perfect flow, an unfolding.

It is happening right now.

Relax.
Trust.

I know where you wish to go and have charted the most direct path. Mighty forces are combining to forward your purpose.

Have faith that you will arrive where you wish to be, and it must be so.

Love,
God

OCTOBER 12

To: You

You stand on a dock gazing out over deep water.

Suddenly you lose your footing and fall in.

Looking around, you don't see a ladder or other way to exit. You're uncertain as to the best way to make shore, and you start to feel afraid.

You have a choice.

You can either flail your arms in panic and risk drowning, or you can use those very same arms to gently tread water. Once you have calmed down and figured out the best direction, you can swim out.

Rather than leaping to action in time of crisis, it is often best to stop, get your bearings, calm yourself, and then proceed.

Remind yourself of this often.
Test it during small challenges, and reach for it during large ones.

Love,
God

OCTOBER 13

To: You

The wind passes over your body. You feel its caress, you sense its presence, and yet you cannot see it.

Although it cannot be seen, you see the wind's effects everywhere in the rustling of leaves, the ripples on the face of the water, and the sheets fluttering gently on the clothesline.

Similarly, although you cannot see me, you can see my effects all around you. Opportunities present themselves. People reach out to love and support you. Problems resolve themselves into improvements for your life.

Beloved, if you could see the wind, your gaze would be upon it rather than the beauty of its effects. If you could see me, your attention would wander away from the goodness I bring.

This day, let every breeze remind you that I am ever-present—surrounding, supporting, and loving you.

Love,
God

OCTOBER 14

To: You

You click the slow motion button on your remote, and the action on your TV slows down.

The actors remain the same.
The plot doesn't change.
The ending doesn't shift.

You have slowed down the speed—nothing else has been altered.

Try pressing the slow motion button on your life.

You feel you need to speed up—to do things faster and faster. You are in a frenetic race to catch up with yourself.

Slow down…move more slowly and deliberately rather than quickly and frantically.

An unhurried, unstressed pace will actually accomplish more, as well as make you calmer and happier.

Love,
God

OCTOBER 15

To: You

It's not my power.
It is the power of your belief.

It's not about believing in me.
It is about believing in an outcome.

My power is constant—it's a given. Think of it as water pressure inside a pipe. The power of your belief turns the handle. In other words, the more you believe, the more abundance flows.

You can sit in front of a faucet all day, but nothing is going to happen until you open the tap—until you believe.

Open the tap. Believe strongly in what you desire, and it must flow to you.

And just as you wouldn't turn off the faucet until your cup is filled, hold your belief steadfast until what you desire is realized.

Love,
God

Flow
OCTOBER 16

To: You

The warmth of spring is replaced by the heat of summer.
Summer's swelter fades into autumn cool.
Autumn slips into winter freeze, which is thawed by the glow of spring.

And the cycle continues.

The earth experiences seasons and so do you. Whatever is happening
for you, it will change.

Accepting the flow of nature allows you to find beauty in each season.
Accepting your present situation allows you to enjoy it if it is pleasant,
    or move more quickly through it if it is not.

This day, seek the beauty in whatever season you find yourself, and know
that it will, in time, flow perfectly into the next.

Love,
God

OCTOBER 17

To: You

You decide on something you wish to eat.
You go to the store and purchase the ingredients.
Arriving home, you wash and prepare everything.
Next, you mix it all together in the right proportions and heat
    it on the stove.

Is the meal ready to be served?
Not yet.

It has to simmer for a while. It is during this time, when you can smell but not yet taste what you have created, that you build up a strong appetite for what's cooking. This hunger guarantees that when all the ingredients have stewed together, your first taste will be astounding.

So relax.

You've done your part, now I'll do mine.

Things are cooking along nicely.
Smells good, doesn't it?

Love,
God

OCTOBER 18

To: You

It is no accident that your word *spirit* comes from the Greek *spiritus*, which means breath.

When you feel connected to the vastness of Spirit, your breathing is deep and calm. When you feel isolated in the scarcity of human existence, your breath becomes rapid and shallow.

If you are feeling disconnected from Spirit, close your eyes and take a few deep breaths, focusing on the feeling of air moving in and out.

Remind yourself that you are always breathing. And you are always and ever will be one with my Spirit.

This day, be aware of your breathing and feel our oneness in Spirit.

Love,
God

OCTOBER 19

To: You

The sun shines, spreading light and heat without regard as to who will be warmed by its rays.

The wind blows, moving windmills and scattering seeds without giving thought as to who will be touched by its breezes.

The rain falls without consideration as to who will be quenched by its drops.

Nature gives what nature has and does not worry if it will be enough. All is provided.

You are one with nature. You need not fear that what you have to give is not enough. Simply give what you have, and it will be plenty.

Love,
God

Flow
OCTOBER 20

To: You

Once you have answers, the questions will often become more complex. This is as it has always been and how it always shall be.

The game you came here to play is to constantly seek better answers—to find the answer that resolves the current situation, to ferret out a solution that leads you to the next step along your path. That is life.

A certain mind is a closed mind.
A questioning mind is an open mind.

You have questions now.
Answers will come.

You have answers now.
Questions will come.

Love,
God

OCTOBER 21

To: You

You are surrounded by angels—loving beings whose greatest joy is to serve and support you.

These angels are disguised as friends, lovers, coworkers, strangers, and especially, those you might call enemies. They are present in your life to bless you with compassion, understanding, and forgiveness. And they are also there to reflect back to you your old wounds so that you might face them, heal them, and leave them behind once and for all.

Angels are my messengers—they serve a divine purpose.

Give thanks for the angels that surround you today. Listen to their guidance, be open to their gifts, embrace their love, and accept their teaching.

This day, be aware that you are in the midst of angels sent by me to bless you.

Love,
God

Flow
OCTOBER 22

To: You

You could spend the rest of your life searching for air.

You could traverse the world looking for air to sustain you and never find it because air cannot be seen.

Yet you are surrounded by it. You are breathing it. You are being sustained by it. Air infuses you.

You would not look for air, so stop looking for me.

When you look for me, you actually look through me and past me. I'm not in some book. I am not in a building. I am all around and within you now. I cannot be seen, only experienced.

This day, cease trying to see me. Experience me instead.

Love,
God

OCTOBER 23

To: You

There is a quiet stream trickling just beneath the surface of your mind.

It is a pure and gentle brook bubbling with peace, and it is flowing this and every moment.

You may visit and drink from this stream whenever you choose.

Simply turn off the noise and distractions of the outside world and turn within.

You need only close your eyes and breathe for a time. Thoughts of the world around you will melt like snow in the noonday sun.

Take time now and throughout this day to visit your quiet, sacred stream.

Love,
God

To: You

When you feel lost and afraid, realize that your thoughts are simply misaligned.

Choose another thought.
Move toward truth.

Know that you are loved, protected, guided, supported, appreciated, cherished, and prospered.

You can never be lost.
You are one with all goodness and light.

Contemplate this truth, and liberate your troubled heart.

Love,
God

OCTOBER 25

To: You

Water explodes from a fountainhead, hangs as if suspended for a second, and then splashes down into the basin of a fountain.

The water pools momentarily before being pumped up to gush once more from the top.

The fountain is not connected to a water supply. The water flows, circulates, and returns in a continuous process.

This is the process for abundance in any and all forms.

Money flows, pools, and returns.
Love flows, pools, and returns.

If there were no water being pumped up, none would cascade from the fountain. There must be giving for there to be receiving.

An abundant pool is ready to drench your life, but it must be pumped up through the action of giving. Give money, and you activate the fountain of money to pour over you. Give love, and love will shower you with its blessings.

Whatever you seek, give it first, and it will—it must—be returned to you.

Love,
God

To: You

Flames travel in one direction—up.

Notice how a candle flame may flicker in the wind but will always realign itself upward.

Although you may feel buffeted about by the winds of life, your direction is like that of the flame—always up. You are moving in the direction of your soul's evolution.

When you feel scorched by the fires of life, realize that they are nothing more than a purification process, burning away what is no longer needed, so that unencumbered you can soar ever higher.

You are a flame. You may flicker, but your direction is always toward the heavens.

Love,
God

OCTOBER 27

To: You

First,

Someone walks a certain path.

Others follow.

To the followers, this is a logical choice.

The person they are following seems to know where to go.

There is confidence and a sense of pride in this person's attitude.

Following this person makes sense.

Next,

Someone steps out of line.

Someone goes in a different direction.

Someone selects a new trail and establishes a path through repeated
steps.

At first the followers scorn the maverick.

The individualist resolutely walks his or her path.

The herd begins to shift as the maverick is followed in ever-greater
numbers.

The process repeats.

Love,
God

OCTOBER 28

To: You

Joy is like breathing.

You cannot take it in all at once.
Nor can you hold on to it forever.

Both joy and breathing come in small, precious moments—moments
that come and then pass.

Experience fully both your breath and your joy, and then release, trusting
more will come.

Feel joy, and then let it pass when it is ready.

So long as you live this life, there will always be a next breath. There will
always be another joyous moment.

Love,
God

OCTOBER 29

To: You

It is during moments of loss that possessions regain their value.

It is during moments of despair that faith is ignited.

It is during moments of hopelessness that new possibilities step from the shadows.

It is during moments of fear that courage makes its stand.

It is during moments of heartbreak that love rushes forth to heal.

It is during moments of quiet that I remind you how divinely powerful you are.

Now is such a moment.

Love,
God

To: You

When you are afraid, you hold your breath. Most fear is about future events, but your body feels the threat as current and breathes more shallowly.

You can lessen stress and lighten your mood by remembering to breathe. Throughout this day, consciously take several deep breaths.

If you catch yourself holding your breath, take several slow, deep breaths to attune yourself again to the natural rhythm of respiration.

Let your breath be a ship that transports you to the calm shores and placid waters of the island of peaceful fulfillment.

Love,
God

OCTOBER 31

To: You

The sun's radiance pours down upon the earth.

Hours later, the earth rotates such that this section of the globe is bathed in the shadows of night.

Where once there was light, there is darkness.
Where once there was vibrancy, there is stillness.
Where once there was warmth, there is coolness.

The sun remains constant, radiating its brilliant power in every direction. The section of your earth has simply turned away for a time to face the blackness of space.

When you feel separated from light, energy, and warmth, they are still fully present. You have simply turned away and are looking into darkness rather than into light.

Turn around, shift your gaze, and you will find that I am present, radiating love, support, compassion, and abundance. I am shining forth with everything you need and everything you desire.

If you are experiencing darkness, know that you are looking at darkness. Look for light, and it will once again dawn and illuminate your life.

Love,
God

NOVEMBER

Appreciate

Gratitude is an elevator transporting you to
 higher and happier levels of life.
Gratitude shifts your focus away from darkness
 and toward the light.
Gratitude transforms cries of woe into exclama-
 tions of joy.
Gratitude sees a mountain of opportunity and
 ignores the foothill of difficulty.
Gratitude awakens the angel of elation and
 vanquishes the demon of despair.
Gratitude raises your vibration, attracting
 to you more for which to be grateful.
Gratitude opens your heart and invokes
 compassion.
Gratitude transforms what is into what can be.
Gratitude is your greatest power for creation.
Gratitude slumbers within you now, awaiting
 your call.

Begin now to count your blessings in earnest,
and you will never finish, for there is far more
to celebrate than there is time for celebration.

NOVEMBER 1

To: You

Look forward with excitement.
Look back with compassion.

Look forward with faith.
Look back with gratitude.

Look forward with wonder.
Look back with understanding.

Look forward with hope.
Look back with forgiveness.

Look forward with confidence.
Look back with reverence.

Love,
God

NOVEMBER 2

To: You

Your human mind will never ever have enough. It is a yawning, gaping, bottomless pit that demands constant nourishment and is never satisfied.

More money! More attention! More love! More, more, more!

How do you escape the mind's incessant howlings for more?

The craving mind is silenced through the application of gratitude. An ongoing checklist of the endless bounty you now possess engages the mind and quiets its pleadings.

This day, place your focus on the many, many things you have for which to be grateful.

Give your mind the pleasant task of counting your endless blessings, and it will cease to wail about the smattering of things you currently lack.

Love,
God

To: You

Imagine if everyone took a marking pen and wrote the word *blessing* in large, bold letters on everything that brings them health, happiness, safety, or joy.

What if you were assigned this task? You would write *blessing* on the faces of your children and friends, on every corner of your home, on your car, on the public servants who provide for you, on the table where you eat your meals.

How different would your day be if you spent it notating every blessing? Imagine how the world would look to you once everyone took up this challenge. If every person on earth wrote *blessing* on everything for which they were grateful, practically everything would bear the inscription *blessing*.

You would see the truth—that you are surrounded by blessings.

And as you went to bed that night, you would look in the mirror and see *blessing* written on your own forehead, for you are indeed a great blessing to many, many people.

This day, grab a pen—even an imaginary one—and play the blessing game.

Love,
God

NOVEMBER 4

To: You

Right where you are is perfect.

Reading this, you may feel an urge to disagree, saying, "Well, if only this were different" or "If only I owned that." And yet a lessening of struggles or an increase in possessions cannot alter the perfection of now.

If you cannot enjoy now, having fewer struggles will not make you
   happy.
If you cannot be fulfilled where you are, neither will you be when you
   possess more objects.

Even when your current struggle abates, your soul will attract another to inspire its growth. When you possess what you currently desire, more wants will crop up.

Such is human life.

This day, remind yourself that you are in the midst of perfection, and let it be so for you.

Love,
God

To: You

When you are ready, you will see.

You will see the goodness that surrounds you when you see the goodness that is within you.

When you see that abundance flows through you, you will experience abundance flowing to you.

When you see that others are one with you, you will see the beauty in your oneness.

When you see that your drama is self-created, you will be free to create a new experience of life.

Are you ready to see and to know?

Is this the day?

Love,
God

NOVEMBER 6

To: You

Have you noticed that when a child is faced with giving away an old toy, the toy suddenly becomes very valuable?

Giving something away increases its value in your mind. This is why it is so important to give to others. When you give—be it money, time, loving attention, or in whatever way you are guided—you begin to appreciate what you have all the more.

Giving money increases your appreciation for money.
Giving time increases your appreciation for time.
Giving compassion increases your appreciation for compassion.

This day, give and it will be given back to you in even greater abundance.

Love,
God

NOVEMBER 7

To: You

Honestly answer the following questions:

Do you ruminate over upsetting experiences from your past?

Do you think frequently about challenges that may happen
in the future?

When you spend time in thoughts that engender pain about the past or fear about the future, you diminish your capacity for joy and happiness in the present.

Be at rest.

The painful experiences from your past are gone. We handled them.

Be at peace.

The frightening experiences you envision in your future may or may
not occur, but if they do, we will handle them as well.

This day, drink in the beauty that is all around you, which can only be experienced in this moment. Do not allow shadows from your past or projections about your future to diminish your appreciation for all the goodness in your life.

Love,
God

Appreciate

November 8

To: You

What do you love?
What brings you joy?
What gives your life meaning?

Once you know clearly the answers to these questions, commit to spending your day doing these things. Today offers a great many chances for you to find love, joy, and meaning by simply participating in your passions.

Coded within your DNA are not only your unique physical characteristics but also your unique desires and tastes, the experience of which brings you joy and fulfillment.

Do you love writing? Make time to write.

Do you enjoy working with your hands? Begin to create something.

Do you find happiness in talking with others? Make a plan now to call or meet with someone.

This day, the only day you have to live, is filled with promise for your greatest fulfillment.

Love,
God

To: You

Depending on where you stand, every exit is also an entrance.

When you take a stand to appreciate everything—not only things that you possess but also the things that are lost to you forever, you channel your life into a never-ending series of wonderful new experiences.

As you live, you will regularly shed people, roles, capabilities, and experiences. As sad as their leaving may be, each passing creates a vacuum for new discovery, growth, and exploration.

This day, give thanks for what has faded from your life. It has left behind memories to make you smile and wisdom to help you thrive.

Love,
God

To: You

Wise shoppers make a list.

Modern superstores carry a dizzying array of products, and without a list to guide you, you might be tempted to pick up something that you don't really want or that might not be good for you.

Your life is a megastore, and you are the shopper. If you walk in without a list, you may spend a great deal of time in the store and, in the end, leave without what you want or, worse, buy something that does not bring you health and happiness.

The solution is to make two lists and stick to them.

First make a list of what you desire, and read it frequently. Remind yourself what you do and do not want. Focus on what you intend to have, and you draw it to you.

Make a second list of things you are grateful for, and read it so as not to be tempted to buy the negativity and bad news bombarding you.

Be a wise shopper in the vast superstore that is the universe. Make your list and stick to it.

Love,
God

Appreciate
NOVEMBER 11

To: You

One of your sacred stories states that I concluded each of the seven days creating the universe by being appreciative—"And God saw that it was good."

Appreciation has powerful creative energy.
Appreciation creates sweetness where once there was bitterness.
Appreciation creates joy where once there was sorrow.
Appreciation creates prosperity where once there was poverty.
Appreciation creates possibilities where once there were limitations.

This day, tap into the infinite creative power of appreciation.

Love,
God

NOVEMBER 12

To: You

Your mind is troubled. You feel that if you were only somehow better, then life would be perfect.

You think that if you were only thin enough, wealthy enough, smart enough, or serene enough, then all would be well.

Because you think this way, fulfillment looms before you on the distant horizon. As you amble forward, the horizon simply moves farther away.

According to your fear-based ego, you will never be good enough. The ego uses this conflict between what you are and what it feels you should be to keep you off balance.

You will find peace when you realize that you will never be enough to satisfy the unrealistic expectations from the chattering voice inside your head.

When you give up the game of trying to be enough, you will realize that right here, right now, exactly as you are, you already are enough.

Love,
God

To: You

As you begin to exhale your last breath, do you want your final thought to be *I figured it out* or *I enjoyed myself*?

You expend so much energy trying to figure your life out that you miss much of life's joy.

Certainly there should be time for introspection. Yes, learning new and better ways to live in this world makes sense. But life is like a wall covered in infinite layers of paint. You may delve beneath the surface of many, but you will never move through them all.

This day, let your activities be directed by what brings you happiness. Release your attachment to figuring yourself and life out.

Give yourself over to that which brings you joy, and be thankful for living this life.

Love,
God

To: You

If you were to make a list of everything that is going well in your life, every blessing you are experiencing and everyone who loves you, you would fill many pages.

If you then made a list of every problem, struggle, and difficult person you are dealing with, you might be surprised to discover how short this list is.

Whenever you are feeling down, do this very thing. Make a list of all that is going well, and then write down everything that challenges you.

This is the surest way to realize how very much you have to appreciate and how little you have to fret about.

And here's something to note: the more you do this, the more you will find your "good" list growing longer and your "bad" list getting shorter.

Love,
God

To: You

Look about you.

See the many great blessings that surround you right now.

There are opportunities to connect with others.
There are new things to be learned.
There is much goodness and abundance.
And there is much fulfilling and rewarding work to be done.

Enjoy what you find, and do what is yours to do.
Disregard the actions or inactivity of others.
What another chooses to do or not do cannot affect you unless you
allow it to do so.

Be open to your ability to augment your journey as you go, and find
peace in being detached.

This day, enjoy your unique world.

Love,
God

To: You

Say "please" and "thank you."

I know the people who guided you through childhood encouraged you to use these words so that you would act politely when dealing with other people. But I want you to understand the transformative power of saying "please" and "thank you."

Say "please"—that is, consciously ask for what you want. Stating your desire sets into motion its manifestation. It clarifies what you wish to draw from the infinite well of the universe.

Say "thank you"—that is, express appreciation for what you have. Saying "thank you" for what you now possess creates a fertile field for cultivating the seeds of your desire. Gratitude for what you currently have opens the doors to what you will very soon have.

Love,
God

To: You

Open your eyes and see.

Let your vision soak in the wonder and beauty all around you, and know that it is a reflection of your soul's own inner splendor.

You are a vibrant, perfect soul that resounds with the spirit of the world.

Harmonize with the perfection surrounding you.

Look for beauty in the landscape, in animals, in the sky, in cities and plains.

See the majestic spirit in each passing face, and know that it is there to remind you of your own magnificence.

Open your eyes to the limitless goodness that is.

Love,
God

To: You

You are deserving of everything you wish to receive.

You question this, and this very uncertainty is what leaves you wanting. Even now you thirst while directly before you is an oasis inviting you to come, slake your desire.

"You are worthy," it says. "Approach, drink deep."

You fear that if you take too much there might be an accounting, and something or someone could be taken from you.

But such is not the case.

As you open yourself to receive more, more will be offered, for such is divine law.

Love,
God

NOVEMBER 19

To: You

I can sum up all transformation for you: give thanks for what is.

Your gratitude for whatever presents itself allows you to see both what you think of as rewards and what you think of as challenges as beautiful and delicate stones that comprise the mosaic of your life.

The beauty and perfection of the mosaic cannot be seen while the stones are, one by one, being put into place. Rather, the magnificent artistic treasure that is your life can be appreciated only in retrospect.

There are many things that have come your way that you would sorely
    miss if they were taken from you.
These things are blessings; be grateful for them.

There are challenges and difficulties that have jarred you awake and
    pushed your soul back onto its path and, in the process, given you
    wisdom and discernment.
These are blessings; be grateful for them.

Give thanks in all things, and life will kneel before you with outstretched arms laden with gifts.

Love,
God

To: You

There is no beach, only individual grains of sand massed together. The beach does not exist apart from the sand.

Similarly, you have no life, as you call it, only moments strewn together in what seems like a succession of events. Each moment is a grain of sand. Without the moment, you have no life. Life can only be measured in moments.

How do you plan to use the moments that will comprise this day? Do you plan for joy and wonder? Are you looking forward to great discoveries and new experiences?

Remember—once the moments are gone, they are like grains of sand washed from the beach forever.

Set an intention now to be fully engaged in whatever you are doing, whatever you are feeling, whatever you are experiencing—be with it fully, knowing it will never be repeated.

Appreciate every grain of sand that is your life.

Love,
God

To: You

Before humans walked this planet, there were trees, soil, rivers, rocks, and animals.

From these and other resources, human beings have made stuff—lots and lots of stuff.

Some of this stuff has made life simpler and healthier, but far too much of it has made life more complicated and distracting.

If your stuff were all gone tomorrow, what would you be left with? In what would you find pleasure and joy?

That which is of real value is beyond your ability to purchase—it is the love and companionship of friends and family.

Possessions bind you through ownership, whereas loving relationships liberate you through mutual appreciation and a desire for what is best for one another.

This day, give thanks not for stuff but for people.

Love,
God

To: You

What you say goes.

Your life is a projection of your thoughts.
But it is your words that give your thoughts creative power.

There is a reason your vocal chords are midway between your brain and your heart. Speak with a thoughtful mind and a compassionate heart, and your world will be practical and loving.

Speak words of appreciation, and you invite more to be appreciated.

When you express appreciation for other people, they give back more of the behaviors you appreciate.

When you express appreciation for life, life finds ways of giving you more for which to be grateful.

What you say goes. Make certain that what you say most often is "thank you," and in so doing, you set into motion the assurance of still more goodness coming your way.

Love,
God

NOVEMBER 23

To: You

Comparing yourself to another person could improve your understanding of yourself...if you fully knew the other person.

However, such a thing is impossible.

What you think you know about someone is actually projections based on limited information. Your mind fills in gaps in your knowledge of someone by painting too perfect a picture. Your idealized view of him or her ensures that you will not measure up.

Compare yourself to no one, for comparisons are impossible. Comparisons are based on differences, and at your core, you are not different from anyone. You are all the same—divine.

Celebrate this day how very much you are like everyone else. You are all humans exploring and enjoying life, doing your best with the resources you have.

This day, celebrate your kinship with all.

Love,
God

To: You

An orchestra conductor attempts to draw the most out of each individual note of a symphony.

Full attention is given to every measure until it melds seamlessly into the next, which then becomes his sole focus. This happens thousands of times during a performance, and all so quickly that patrons take no notice.

The result of the maestro's single-minded attention to each note is a performance of beauty and power.

You are the conductor, and every moment is a note in the symphony of your life. To whatever extent you can, focus full, loving, appreciative attention on whatever is currently transpiring.

Then release it.

Just as an orchestra would not hold a single note indefinitely, regardless of how pleasant it sounds, let go of each moment when it has passed, and open yourself up to the next.

As you glide gratefully from moment to moment, from note to note, you create a beautiful and enduring melody.

Love,
God

To: You

Lack is more than not having enough of this or that.

Lack is a way of living—it is a mental condition that causes people to dwell upon things that they feel are missing rather than focusing on what is present.

You experience lack externally because you experience it internally. "Never enough" in your mind leads to "never enough" in your world.

Shift from lack to abundance by remembering the twin meanings of the word *appreciate:*
1. To be grateful for something or someone
2. To add value

When you show appreciation, what you appreciate increases in value.

This day, let appreciation take you by the hand and walk you from a world of lack into a world of abundance.

Love,
God

To: You

For the love you receive,
For the joy you feel,
For the knowledge you gain every day,
For the life you are fortunate enough to live,
For the talents and unique abilities you alone possess,

For these things and so much more, give thanks.

Giving thanks magnifies your awareness of your blessings, bringing
   you joy.
Giving thanks expands your capacity for goodness, allowing you
   to receive even greater gifts.

Give thanks often. It's not for my benefit that you express gratitude, but
for your own. As you do, you will be regularly reminded, in your own
words, just how truly great your life is.

Then be prepared for it to get even better.

Love,
God

To: You

Every snowflake is truly unlike every other, and here's why:

Each snowflake is formed around a unique, microscopic dust particle floating in the atmosphere. It is created at a different altitude, at a slightly different temperature, and with varying degrees of moisture than every other flake.

The snowflake then rises and falls and is blown to and fro through the air hundreds, if not thousands, of times, collecting slightly more or less water in a billion, billion possible combinations.

This can go on for weeks before the snowflake is heavy enough to join hundreds of millions of others falling from the sky to blanket the landscape in white.

A great combination of factors makes each snowflake unique.

An even more staggering combination of elements called forth the distinct and perfect individual that you are.

No snowflake is any more or less perfect than another.
The same is true for people.

This day, give thanks for what makes you uniquely who you are.

Love,
God

NOVEMBER 28

To: You

From the prism-like beauty of dewdrops refracting the morning sun, to the shimmering majesty of an ever-changing ocean, there is beauty everywhere.

Nature is beautiful in whatever stage she finds herself.
People are beautiful, from the ebony-skinned Masai of the African Serengeti to the pale-complexioned farmers living in the Irish foothills.

Beauty abounds, and as you seek beauty, you find her.

When you set your mind to find and savor beauty, she stands before you, arms open, inviting you to gaze in delight upon her transcendent grandeur.

This day, be on the watch for beauty, for there is much to see that is beautiful.

And remember, my precious child, you are able to behold this beauty because it is a reflection of the perfect beauty that shines from within you.

Seek the beauty that awaits you in your mirror as well as in your world.

Love,
God

Appreciate

NOVEMBER 29

To: You

Far beneath your feet is molten rock.
Stretching above your head is the void of space.

You could not live in either the molten rock below or the vacuum of space above. Here in the middle, between the two, you are in the best place possible.

Do you see that the same is true regarding time? You are best suited to live here, now, in the middle, between the past and the future.

Do not dwell in the molten rock of the past.
Venture not into the void that is the future.
Ground yourself in the present with expressions of gratitude.

Here you are, for now.
This is where you belong.
Be grateful.

Love,
God

To: You

All relationships are a mirror of one's self. In another person, you see your own inner expression reflected back to you.

Seeing yourself in someone else may present itself as love and admiration. It may also come out as stress and conflict.

The conflict is neither in the relationship nor in the other person.

Rather, it is in you.

A relationship is a divine appointment. It is not only divinely arranged; it is a meeting of the divine itself, because you are both perfect expressions of Spirit.

When you come together with someone, and you accept any subsequent discord as your own issue to be resolved, you are able to release the difficulty and transform the relationship.

This day, give thanks for your connections with others and for everything these relationships bring up, calling you deeper into your own wholeness.

Love,
God

December

flourish

Within you burns the light of the ages—a
brilliance that rivals the stars.

Powerful enough to illuminate the world's
darkness, this light never fades, never dwindles;
it shines eternal.

The light may be obscured, but it can never
be extinguished.

Cease to live a shadow life, allowing only a
silhouette to be cast.

Instead, flourish. Let my light shine through
you, for this is the highest demonstration of life.

December 1

To: You

A man owned a coin.

Throughout the man's life, the coin remained nestled in the corner of his pocket. Although the coin became dirty, encrusted with lint, and nearly rubbed smooth, the man clung to it.

When the man died, the coin was put into the pocket of his burial clothes and placed, along with his body, into the ground.

The coin's value was lost because it was never used.

There are words that you plan to use someday—words of love, forgiveness, apology, appreciation, and compassion.

One day, perhaps this day, you will be buried along with those words, and they will become worthless.

Share your words today. Tell others how you feel. Use your words and let their value multiply. Then watch how those around you begin to flourish.

Love,
God

December 2

To: You

A surfer doesn't seek out a small, predictable wave.

No, she seeks a wave that pushes the limits of her surfing capacity—one that keeps her on the edge, allows her to feel the thrill of the challenge and the unpredictability of the ride.

Your soul is a surfer.
Life is its ocean.

Your soul seeks a ride that is stimulating—one that calls forth its potential while simultaneously melding it with the power of the wave.

Right now, you are lying on your board and paddling out into a wave that you call Today. You may feel excited, anxious, or a combination of the two.

If you make it all the way to the shore while standing on your board, or if you fall partway, pat yourself on the back for trying. Know that your soul is beckoning another wave called Tomorrow that is, even now, moving over the horizon to greet you.

Surf's up! Enjoy the ride.

Love,
God

DECEMBER 3

To: You

How will you dance?

You can dance as you have been instructed.
You can dance preplanned steps and patterns.
You can dance your version of what is popular.
You can dance as you have seen others dance.
You can dance as you have always danced before.
You can dance in an attempt to tempt, please, or satisfy someone else.

Or you can dance by giving yourself over to the music.
You can dance by surrendering to the rhythm.
You can dance by flowing with the energy that pulsates within your
    being.
You can dance by feeling your heart glide in time with your feet.
You can dance without regard to how your steps will be interpreted
    by others.

The music of life is playing.
How will you dance?

Love,
God

DECEMBER 4

To: You

Gaze deeply into the mirror, and see me looking back.
Look into the eyes of your child, and my love is reflected your way.
Seek to understand why a complex knot of troubles has unraveled,
      and you will find my hands.
Watch the playful antics of a puppy, and witness my exuberance.
Notice the helpful guidance of a friend, and experience my presence.
Listen to the melodic strains of music, and hear my voice.
Savor the taste of your favorite foods, and know that I am at once
      the farmer, the chef, and the server.

For such I am.

Ah, but can you look into the eyes of a defiant stranger and find me?
Can you hear a tale of tragedy and know that in this, too, I am present?
Can you watch as something you treasured comes to an end and know
      that you are being supported, not abandoned, by me?

I am the light.
Shine me into your perceived darkness, and it will withdraw.

Always.

Love,
God

DECEMBER 5

To: You

Be childlike.

A child enjoys each moment as it presents itself.
A child asks for what is needed.
A child seeks out new experiences.

Children have one priority—to have fun.

Have fun. You have no idea how long your sojourn on earth will last. When you and I sit together face to face, I want to hear you tell lots and lots of stories about how much fun you had in life.

This day, find the many ways I have presented you to have fun.

Do something you enjoy doing.
Spend time with people you love.
Laugh for no particular reason.
Take a new route home.
Skip in the park.

Express the child that is you by having fun.

Love,
God

DECEMBER 6

To: You

Consider your commonly uttered phrase "Take time."

"I've got to take time to relax," you say.
"I've got to take time to exercise," you declare.

Your words are powerful—they concretize your thoughts into reality.
Therefore, consider a powerful shift in your phrasing. Never "take time."

Time is not something to be taken. It is not something you withdraw.
Rather, time is something you invest.

Invest time in your family.
Invest time in your hobbies.
Invest time in your work.
Invest time in exercise.
Invest time in silent reflection.

Things that are taken are fleeting and soon depleted. Investments, on the other hand, pay dividends.

Reshape your concept of time. Cease to take time; rather, begin to invest it as your most precious asset.

Love,
God

DECEMBER 7

To: You

A gift sits before you. Neither the size of the box nor the wrapping paper provides a hint as to what lies inside.

What could the gift be? Is it fun, functional, educational, or a smattering of all three?

Will it require assembly?

Is the gift something you will enjoy for years to come, or is it something you will accept with a halfhearted smile and put in a closet where it will soon be forgotten?

Today is such a gift—that is why it is called the present.

This day will be fun, challenging, educational, and some assembly will be required. But if you give yourself fully to it, today will be a gift you will remember for the rest of your life.

Love,
God

DECEMBER 8

To: You

If you wish to feel happy, be kind.

Hard-wired within your soul is a powerful drive to help other people. Even the smallest act of kindness reminds you of this and causes you to enjoy life all the more.

You will have dozens of opportunities to practice kindness today:
Hold the door for someone.
Refrain from making a negative comment.
Let someone go ahead of you in traffic.
Help carry someone's burden.
Give to a homeless person.
Smile unceasingly into a frowning face.
Do a small task for someone.
Call a friend with the intention of listening more than you speak.

If you pick up stones of kindness along the pathway of life, you experience a happy journey.

Love,
God

DECEMBER 9

To: You

Have you ever noticed that being around a person with what you would call an accent causes you, in time, to begin to speak like him or her?

Human beings have a subconscious connection that causes them to move into sync with those they are with.

Choose carefully, therefore, with whom you share your time.

Whenever two people come together, their energy begins to synchronize as one person's vibration slows down, one person's energy speeds up, or there is a combination of the two. This exchange of energy can leave a lingering effect.

Surround yourself with people you want to be more like. In time, you will begin to vibrate at the same frequency, and your life will match that vibration.

And don't feel guilty for choosing not to associate with some people. Instead, send them love.

Everyone deserves your love.
Not everyone deserves your time.

Love,
God

DECEMBER 10

To: You

You invest so much time in your to-do lists, your programs, your commitments, your plans, and your regimens. You stress and fret that you are not getting enough things done or that you are not doing some things well enough.

C'mon, relax—have fun.

When it's all said and done, your lists of tasks will not have mattered. The number of items you accomplished will not bring you satisfaction. What is truly important are the times you enjoyed yourself.

It is not irresponsible to have fun.
It is irresponsible to let your life pass without being enjoyed.

Now, what sounds like fun today?

Love,
God

DECEMBER 11

To: You

A boat moving through the ocean will face a variety of waves—some will be small, others quite large. Some will have deep swells; others will be shallow.

How the boat approaches the waves is critical. If a large enough wave strikes the boat broadside, the craft could capsize. However, if the captain turns the bow directly into the oncoming wave and faces it head-on, the vessel will glide through.

As life's events send waves rippling in your direction, don't turn away, or they may jostle you about and threaten to tip you over. Instead, turn to face life's waves directly and plow through them.

Right now, some sort of wave is either striking your hull or moving in your direction.

You are the captain of the ship that is your life. This day, face your waves head-on.

Love,
God

December 12

To: You

Consider the life rings of a tree. The rings start small and become increasingly larger as the tree matures.

After decades of life, a skinny sapling develops into a towering giant whose branches canopy the sky. It took many years—many rings—for this tree to reach the heavens. Its expansive growth did not occur in one large ring.

No, there were hundreds, perhaps thousands, of rings, each taking its time to form, and each necessary for the rings that came after.

Rushing growth never works. A tree is built a year at a time; a life is built a day at a time.

Add a ring of growth to your life today—even a small one. Then tomorrow add another. Soon you will find you have become a towering giant.

Love,
God

DECEMBER 13

To: You

Freedom isn't something that is granted.
Freedom stems from a decision to be free.

When you become resolute in your intention to be free, outer experiences must shift and realign. Soon you find yourself liberated.

If you feel bound to relationships, employment, past experiences, habits, perceived limitations, or anything else, stop railing against what you believe holds you captive.

This only strengthens the bond.

Your ability to decide is the fount from which all freedom flows. Simply decide that you are now free, and hold a vision of liberation.

When you claim your freedom, I will realign both you and your world, and very soon this will be your reality.

Love,
God

DECEMBER 14

To: You

When you watch an accomplished athlete, you are seeing someone who has invested thousands of hours in practice and preparation.

No athlete walks onto the gridiron, the court, or the diamond without daily practice.

The same is true for someone who seeks to become more spiritually enlightened. It takes a daily investment of time in prayer, contemplation, and meditation.

Superstar athletes are born with the same muscles you have. They have just developed them.

The great spiritual masters have the same mind and heart you possess. They have simply cultivated their attunement with Spirit.

A little prayer and some time in quiet meditation will, in time, make you the spiritual gold medalist you were born to become.

Love,
God

DECEMBER 15

To: You

You are seated in a comfortable room on a pleasant day. You feel happy and content.

Suddenly a bird flies in through an open window and begins to dart around your head. Soon another bird joins in, and the two repeatedly flit around, scratching and pecking you.

More birds fly in through the window and join the fray. Before long, dozens of aerial marauders are assaulting you. You wave your arms frantically, trying to shoo them off. You become consumed with protecting yourself and deflecting the attacks.

Now imagine if the window were closed. Birds would strike the glass and, dazed but unhurt, fly away, leaving you unmolested.

Negative thoughts that come into your mind are like these birds. They attack you. They encroach upon your solemnity. The more one thought attacks, the more vulnerable you become to others.

This day, fill the room of your mind to overflowing with thoughts of love and gratitude, and you will close the window to negative thoughts. They may strike the panes, but you will be free from their assaults.

Love,
God

December 16

To: You

Some go to a temple to find me.
Along the way, they pass me by.

While in their sacred space, they are reminded of me.
Then they fail to take me with them when they leave.

Enjoy your churches, temples, synagogues, mosques, and other holy places. Just remember that I am equally in the movie theater, along the interstate, in your family gathering, at your job, with you and your beloved.

Most important, I am with you right now, loving you and holding you close, for you are my dearest treasure.

Love,
God

To: You

You want everything to be perfect—no problems, no challenges, no struggles.

You also know that it feels wonderful to help someone, right?

Imagine, then, if there were no problems, no challenges, and no struggles for you or anyone else. How would you get that great feeling from helping others if there were nothing anyone needed?

I have supplied all the solutions to solve everyone's problems. The solutions are you and every other person I have lovingly created. When I did so, I encoded within your very DNA a craving for the pleasure you get from helping other people.

It's a perfect system.

Know that one of the reasons you experience challenges is so others can feel good by helping you through them.

Offer help to others and be blessed.
Receive help from others and bless them.

Love,
God

DECEMBER 18

To: You

When you walk into a church, cathedral, mosque, synagogue, or other
house of worship, you remember.
When you stroll through nature, you remember.
When you take time to pray, you remember.

You remember that there is a sacredness that surrounds and enfolds
you at all times.

Wherever you stand, you stand upon holy ground.

There is no place more sacred than where you are.
There is no time more holy than this moment.

You stand at the causal point of all creation. Every moment is a time
of spiritual beginning as well as spiritual fulfillment.

Remember that no matter where you are, you stand at the epicenter
of God.

Love,
God

December 19

To: You

Give, and shift your focus from your own challenges to making someone else's life better.

Give, and affirm your abundance, knowing that you are prosperous enough to be able to give.

Give, and see how what you give returns to you magnified.

Your eternal light burns brightly, calling you forth from the darkness of fear and lack. That light is generous giving.

Notice what and to whom you readily give and from whom you withhold. Then realize it is your unwillingness to give to some that diminishes your capacity to receive.

Give freely, and you will receive abundantly.

Love,
God

DECEMBER 20

To: You

You put forth effort to make yourself more attractive. You exercise your body, apply makeup and creams to your skin, style your hair, and carefully select what you wear.

As attractive as you become externally, your appearance will never exceed your internal beauty.

As much gentleness, love, compassion, happiness, and empathy as you have thus far mined from your inner quarry, there are truckloads to be discovered, extracted, polished, and shared.

Take as much time to cultivate your inner beauty as you do your outer appearance. Seek out the exquisiteness and style to be found within, and offer it to the world.

Love,
God

DECEMBER 21

To: You

Two hungry birds perch side by side on a fence post.

Insects swarm behind the pair. Sensing their presence, one bird turns around and snatches the bugs out of the air, savoring his meal.

Facing as before, the other bird snaps his beak ineffectively at the empty air.

"What are you doing?" asks the first.
"Eating," replies the second. "But for some reason, I'm still hungry."
"You are reaching out where there is nothing," offers the first bird with a gentle smile.
"I don't care," declares the second bird, "This is the direction I am facing; this is where I will eat."

If you are reaching for love, understanding, companionship, peace, friendship, and prosperity but grasping only empty air, you may need to face a new direction.

This day, seek what you desire only where it is present. Turn in a new direction and be filled.

Love,
God

DECEMBER 22

To: You

When you look at a graph of a company that has experienced rapid positive growth, you will note occasional dips in its progress along the way.

A straight line to success is not realistic because it takes time for the company to adjust to being a larger, more successful version of itself.

The same is true as you grow into your divine nature. There will be days, even weeks, when you get it—you will feel connected, blissful, attuned to everyone and everything. Then there will be dips. You will feel alone, afraid, and disconnected.

If you can know that the times of fullness are the truth of who you are, they will grow in number.

If you will remember that the times of feeling disconnected are just spiritual growing pains, they will pass, and you will spiral higher.

This day, whether you are on an upswing or in a dip, accept where you are and know that it is all part of growing into the full expression of the divine master you are.

Love,
God

To: You

If something doesn't go your way, you might say "See?" as in:
"See? I can't do it!"
"See? I knew things wouldn't work out!"
"See? I'm simply no good!"

When you say "See?" in this manner, you are seeking external verification that you are stuck, lacking, incapable, and undeserving. This, you feel, excuses you from trying to make things better.

Stop saying "See?" to get other people to agree with your perceived limitations.

Rather, see!

See that together we can do anything.
See that I have always borne you through every challenge.
See that you are loved and appreciated.

And don't pray to me about your limitations.
I see only your potential.

Love,
God

DECEMBER 24

To: You

What you have to say is important—don't hold back.

The words that linger between your mind and your tongue are just what are needed right now.

Today, there is something that you feel guided, yet reluctant, to say.

Know that what you feel inspired to say is going to create an important shift and that you are going to be glad you spoke up.

Listen for that stirring in your mind that seeks expression, take a deep breath, and speak.

Love,
God

DECEMBER 25

To: You

The divine is fully shaped into a human life.

A savior is born into the world.

Humanity rejoices for the living Master.

The one that has been written about has come.

There have been many prophets, many great teachers, and many whose messages have delivered others from suffering and spread love and compassion.

My divine one, none of these spiritual masters is more important to me than you. As you celebrate the anointed ones that came before you, remember that you, too, are my dearly beloved.

Love,
God

DECEMBER 26

To: You

People instinctively bind together in communities for safety, support, fun, and mutual benefit.

Living in community is healthy and natural. However, thinking, acting, and believing just like everyone else is not.

A cow may follow the herd to nutritious grazing, or it may follow the herd into harm's way.

A mass of people doing the same thing is no indication that it is the best thing.

Think for yourself.
Make your own choices.

This day, question the direction of the human herd and discern your own path.

Love,
God

December 27

To: You

Within you now is the child that you once were.
Within you now is the teen that you left behind.
And within you now is the adult that you are.

At times you will act like a child, at others like a teen, and still others like an adult.

The child may want to play. However, the child may also feel shy, petulant, or needy.

The teen may want to experience something new and exciting. The teen may also be demanding, self-centered, and rebellious.

The adult may feel confident and certain. The adult may also feel overwhelmed and stressed.

When the negative side of your child, teen, or adult self appears, invite the positive side of another.

For example, if you feel stressed (adult), take time to play (child). If you feel needy (child), try something new and interesting (teen).

The best of you at any age exists within you at every age. Summon it forth and be your best.

Love,
God

December 28

To: You

As you watch a train glide by, what do you notice?

You notice the cars, right? Watching a train is to notice the size, shape, and motion of the railway cars. When you look at a train, you don't focus on the space between the cars.

The space is not the train.
The cars are the train.

Why then, when you consider your life, do you focus on what you do not have rather than on what you do possess?

To focus upon that which is missing creates dissatisfaction.
To focus upon that which is missing dismisses joy.
To focus upon that which is missing is not to focus at all.

This day, put your attention on what you have rather than what you perceive to be lacking.

Don't miss the train.

Love,
God

DECEMBER 29

To: You

You've overcome thousands of problems.
As a problem shows up, you solve it.

Why then do you still feel a knot of dread when a problem arises? Why does your mind not stay quiet and confident, knowing that this, like all previous challenges, will be resolved?

Life is about your soul's growth, and growth comes from overcoming that which seems difficult.

If you felt confident as you faced a problem, it would not seem difficult, and your soul, which thrives on growth, would be bored and simply attract still larger issues for you to deal with.

Be grateful, therefore, that you have mild amnesia as to how problems are solved, or else you would find yourself with even greater challenges.

The daunting specter of problems inspires you to call into play even more of your divine power and to grow into fuller expressions of spirit.

Love,
God

DECEMBER 30

To: You

Do not wait for others to acknowledge you.

Do not wait until you are ready—you may never be.

Announce your presence to the world.

Step boldly into life now, this day.

Speak your truth.
Walk your path.
Deliver your message.
Offer your gifts.

Let life resound with your greatness.

You have arrived.

Let your light fully shine.

Love,
God

December 31

To: You

If you hear the call and do not answer, it is as if it were never issued.

If you see the summit and do not begin to climb, you will never stand upon its surface.

If you feel guided and do not follow your inspiration, it will slip into the past.

If you see your ideal and do not claim it as your own, it will hover forever beyond your grasp.

If you feel called to improve the lot of humanity but take no action, your contribution will be nil.

Nothing is more powerful than opening the spigot and allowing your own divinity to pour out, drenching the parched earth with love, acceptance, peace, forgiveness, understanding, enthusiasm, and compassion.

You are the one you are waiting for.

You are my personal emissary into this world at this time.

Express the greatness that you are, and in so doing, inspire others to follow your example.

Love,
God

ACKNOWLEDGMENTS

God inspired me and gave me the words to craft these devotionals. This daily task has brought me immeasurable personal growth and satisfaction, and I am eternally grateful.

Lia Bowen served as selections editor for this book. This cumulative work is as much her vision as it is mine. I love you, Lia, and I'm proud of you.

Julia Roller took this diamond in the rough and, through skillful editing, polished it into a gem. Julia, you are a joy and a real talent.

David Kopp and the extraordinary people at Convergent Books are my partners in this divine journey. You are stars in the publishing firmament.

Steve Hanselman has, for more than half a decade, been my agent, my advisor, and my friend. I truly value our relationship.

ABOUT THE AUTHOR

Internationally best-selling author Will Bowen grew up haunting the hallways of his neighborhood church in Columbia, South Carolina. After school and on weekends, Will would sometimes sneak into the church to feel the presence of God in that hallowed space.

Bowen was raised Presbyterian but became Baptist as a teenager to win favor with the family of his first girlfriend. In later years, he considered himself an agnostic atheist—that is, he was unsure which God *not* to believe in. Today, Bowen says, "I've found my way back to the feeling of sitting alone with God in that old church, and my goal is to share that feeling with everyone."

In 2006, Bowen founded A Complaint Free World, which has touched the lives of more than ten million people in 106 countries. He is the author of *A Complaint Free World* and *Happy This Year!* among other titles. Bowen's books have sold millions of copies, and he has been featured on *Oprah,* NBC's *Today* show, *CBS Sunday Morning, Fox News, ABC World News Tonight,* as well as in *People* magazine, *O, The Oprah Magazine, Chicken Soup for the Soul,* and *The Wall Street Journal.*

Will Bowen lives with his wife Marti, daughter Lia, and dog Jake on a small lake near Kansas City, Missouri.